Heavenly Encounters

~ WITNESSING HEAVEN ~

True Stories of Transformation from
Near-Death Experiences

Heavenly Encounters

EDITORS OF GUIDEPOSTS

Heavenly Encounters

Published by Guideposts Books & Inspirational Media
100 Reserve Road, Suite E200
Danbury, CT 06810
Guideposts.org

ACKNOWLEDGMENTS

Every attempt has been made to credit the sources of copyrighted material used in this book. If any such acknowledgment has been inadvertently omitted or miscredited, receipt of such information would be appreciated.

Scripture quotations marked (ESV) are taken from the *Holy Bible, English Standard Version.* Copyright © 2001 by Crossway Bibles, a division of Good News Publishers. Used by permission. All rights reserved.

Scripture quotations marked (KJV) are taken from the *King James Version of the Bible.*

Scripture quotations marked (NASB) are taken from the *New American Standard Bible.* Copyright © 1960, 1962, 1963, 1968, 1971, 1972, 1973, 1975, 1977, 1995 by The Lockman Foundation, La Habra, California. Used by permission.

Scripture quotations marked (NIV) are taken from *The Holy Bible, New International Version.* Copyright © 1973, 1978, 1984, 2011 by Biblica, Inc. Used by permission of Zondervan. All rights reserved worldwide. zondervan.com

Scripture quotations marked (NKJV) are taken from *The Holy Bible, New King James Version.* Copyright © 1982 by Thomas Nelson.

Scripture quotations marked (NLT) are from the *Holy Bible, New Living Translation.* Copyright © 1996, 2004, 2007 by Tyndale House Foundation. Used by permission of Tyndale House Publishers Inc., Carol Stream, Illinois. All rights reserved.

Cover design by Pamela Walker, W Design Studio
Interior design by Pamela Walker, W Design Studio
Cover photo by Dreamstime
Typeset by Aptara, Inc.

ISBN 978-1-959633-99-0 (hardcover)
ISBN 978-1-959633-90-7 (softcover)
ISBN 978-1-959633-91-4 (ebook)

Printed and bound in the United States of America
10 9 8 7 6 5 4 3 2 1

So this is what the Sovereign LORD says:
　"See, I lay a stone in Zion, a tested stone,
　　a precious cornerstone for a sure foundation;
　the one who relies on it
　　will never be stricken with panic."

Isaiah 28:16 (NIV)

CONTENTS

INTRODUCTION

My sheep hear my voice, and
I know them, and they follow me.
I give them eternal life, and they will never perish,
and no one will snatch them out of my hand.

John 10:27-28 (ESV)

The stories of people who claim to have traveled to heaven and back vary. A near-death experience, or NDE, has been defined by the *Merriam-Webster Dictionary* as "an occurrence in which a person comes very close to dying and has memories of a spiritual experience (such as meeting dead friends and family members or seeing a white light) during the time when death was near."

The Bible doesn't record any cases of NDEs, but in the book of Acts, we learn about Stephen, the first martyr of the church and one of the first deacons in the Bible. Steven was a faithful man who believed that Jesus came to fulfill God's promises. Acts 7:55–56 records Stephen's glimpse of heaven as he is being charged by an angry mob moments before he is killed.

But he, being full of the Holy Spirit, gazed into heaven and saw the glory of God, and Jesus standing at the right hand of God, and said, "Look! I see the heavens opened and the Son of Man standing at the right hand of God!" (NKJV)

Through Stephen's example of deep faith and belief that life on earth cannot compare to the joys of heaven, we, too, can learn to speak boldly about the afterlife. For the people who share their stories in this book, the presence of God in heaven was as real to them as it was to Stephen.

A Love that Won't Let Go

Although the Bible doesn't mention NDEs, it does provide support for them through the abundance of verses centered on God's enduring love in both life and death.

God's never-ending divine love flows throughout the stories in *Heavenly Encounters*. Alma Blasquez experienced a love so intense that she longed to remain in the light of heaven's gate. But she sensed that her work on earth was not done and was swiftly sent back to continue on in a new walk steeped in love and compassion. Bud Evans was wounded in battle and almost lost his life, but as he was between this world and heaven, he experienced a love greater than he'd ever known and was also gifted with a vision of a future he never imagined possible for himself.

As Pastor Andrew Garcia was on the brink of death, he learned not only about the magnitude of God's love, but also about the importance of focusing on the small but sacred daily moments of love available to us all. For Jeffrey Coggins, his NDE helped him to see that God has been next to him during his whole life, even during many painful struggles in his youth, and that God will never leave him no matter his challenges in the future.

Forgiveness. Compassion. Abiding love. A peace that passes all understanding. Inexplicable joy. Bright lights. Seeing loved ones who had passed on. Visions of life—past, present, and future. These are just a few of the hallmarks of the heavenly encounters experienced by people who have journeyed to the brink of death, only to be given an opportunity for new life.

Could it be that the reason people have near-death experiences is so that they can bring a slice of heaven back to earth and share it with their family, friends, and loved ones and with the world?

The end of the Lord's Prayer reads, "Thy kingdom come, Thy will be done in earth, as it is in heaven." Matthew 6:10 (KJV)

In earth, as it is in heaven.

Bringing the kingdom of heaven to earth could be perceived as the work of every believer. Loving one's neighbor, helping others, spreading God's Word. But what can we learn from those precious souls who have endured an accident or an illness that brought them to the glorious gates of heaven and then back to life on earth?

Each near-death experience is unique, but a renewed faith in God is the tie that binds many such stories together. A faith that washes away anger and the lingering bondage of unforgiveness. Each person profiled here emerges with a greater love of God and humankind, as well as a deeper understanding that our connections to our loved ones are eternal, whether the loved ones are on earth or in heaven.

Having withstood unimaginable fear, pain, and anguish, Alma, Bud, Andrew, and Jeffrey were transformed and learned that everything they experienced was for a greater purpose. As it says in Romans 8:28 (KJV): "And we know that all things work together for good to them that love God, to them who are the called according to his purpose." As these four discovered through their near-death experiences, their home, like ours, is in heaven.

God's Glorious Promise of Heaven

By C. Hope Flinchbaugh

The heavens declare the glory of God,
and the sky above proclaims his handiwork.

Psalm 19:1 (ESV)

Streets of gold, beautiful gates, and jeweled walls. These are just a few of the phrases many of us have heard to describe heaven. Perhaps the bigger questions, though, are these: Is heaven real? Will I see my departed loved one again in heaven? What is heaven really like?

Theologian Jonathan Edwards said, "To go to heaven, fully to enjoy God, is infinitely better than the most pleasant accommodations here." Other theologians as well as writers, philosophers, and scholars have shared their thoughts about heaven—what it is, what it looks like, and who will greet us when we get there. But nowhere is heaven more exalted than in the Bible. Although the number of times heaven is mentioned in the Bible varies by translation, it is safe to say it appears hundreds of times.

What the Bible Reveals about Heaven

The Bible gives us some beautiful descriptions of heaven, a spectacular place filled with joy and wonder.

Perhaps none is more awe-inspiring than what the apostle John wrote in the book of Revelation. John peered into heaven and the throne room of God in his visions. His descriptions of the wonder and beauty that await us in heaven are dazzling.

> Then the angel showed me the river of the water of life, bright as crystal, flowing from the throne of God and of the Lamb through the middle of the street of the city; also, on either side of the river, the tree of life with its twelve kinds of fruit, yielding its fruit each month. The leaves of the tree were for the healing of the nations. No longer will there be anything accursed, but the throne of God and of the Lamb will be in it, and his servants will worship him. They will see his face, and his name will be on their foreheads. And night will be no more. They will need no light of lamp or sun, for the Lord God will be their light, and they will reign forever and ever. (Revelation 22:1–5, ESV)

In many ways, the Bible could be considered heaven's discovery guidebook. Look at what these Scriptures tell us that we can expect when we arrive in our heavenly home.

- **Heaven is eternal.** "For we know that if the tent that is our earthly home is destroyed, we have a building from God, a house not made with hands, eternal in the heavens." (2 Corinthians 5:1, ESV)

- **Heaven is joyful.** "In your presence there is fullness of joy; at your right hand are pleasures forevermore." (Psalm 16:11, ESV)
- **Heaven is light.** "He has delivered us from the domain of darkness and transferred us to the kingdom of his beloved Son." (Colossians 1:13, ESV)
- **Heaven is full of our friends and loved ones.** "You have come to the assembly of God's firstborn children, whose names are written in heaven. You have come to God himself, who is the judge over all things. You have come to the spirits of the righteous ones in heaven who have now been made perfect." (Hebrews 12:23, NLT)

What Happens when We Die

While we look forward to heaven, it is only natural to wonder what it will be like to transition from our earthly life to a place of eternity. The Bible tells us that when a person dies, the body of clay becomes rigid and the breath of life, God's breath, leaves the person's body at the point of death. If that separation is permanent, then the body returns to the dust from which it was made and the soul or spirit, the real person who lived inside that body, returns to God.

Then shall the dust return to the earth as it was: and the spirit shall return unto God who gave it. (Ecclesiastes 12:7, KJV)

The book of Genesis tells us that after God formed Adam's body from the dust of the earth, God leaned down and breathed into Adam's nose. At that moment, Adam woke up! He came alive and became a living person. When Adam died hundreds of years later, Adam's spirit returned to God and his body stayed below on earth.

I liken this to the force of a magnet. At the time of death, the earth is a magnet that keeps the clay body clinging to its origin, the dust of the ground. God's breath is a magnet that draws our spirit back up to its origin—God in heaven. Our body's life source is the breath of God. When our breath leaves our body, our spirit naturally leaves and returns to God, our source of life.

Our body's life source is the breath of God.

Yet there have been times when people have had a cardiac event, have been close to death, or have had a traumatic event that allowed them to journey to heaven only to return to their earthly body, a phenomenon known as a near-death experience.

What Is a Near-Death Experience?

One doctor made the topic of the afterlife and the experience of dying his personal study. When Raymond Moody, MD, PhD, published his book *Life After Life* in 1975, the subject of what happens to us after death drew the attention of medical professionals, scientists, and everyday people into the public spectrum. In fact, it was Dr. Moody who first coined the term *near-death experience* (NDE) that we use today in the general study of the stories of people who passed through a clinical death and returned to tell others about their experience or vision of the afterlife.

Dr. Moody's intention was to unravel the mystery of life after death and, in the process, find commonalities in stories experienced by people who never met one another. The subject of what happens after death had not been approached objectively before Moody's book was published, but visions of heaven and near-death experiences have been recorded throughout history.

Dr. Moody defines an NDE as "a patterned experience people have after dying or almost dying." He goes on to say that while "no two NDEs are exactly the same, there are striking commonalities."[1]

People oftentimes leave their body and look down on it from above as someone works to resuscitate them. Many testify of passing through a long tube or dark tunnel. Eventually they see light at the end of the tunnel and travel toward the light, flying, not walking, and sometimes accompanied by an angel. Upon arrival in heaven, some see Jesus. Others see deceased loved ones and even talk to them.

While no two NDEs are exactly the same, there are striking commonalities.

Interestingly, Dr. Moody does not see life after death as a scientific question, but considers it a philosophical and religious question. Scientists form facts by consistently observing a topic. If one leans toward a more scientific proof, NDE studies reveal that there are consistent occurrences or patterned experiences that are witnessed by people who have had an NDE. Research by Dr. Moody has shown that even young children have testified to some or all of the same six stages of a near-death experience (see the sidebar on pages 6–7).

The Six Stages of a Near-Death Experience

From tunnels to pearly gates, near-death experiences are amazingly consistent. Here are the six stages most frequently reported by those who have undergone them.

1. OUT OF BODY—An NDE typically starts with a sense of peace. Survivors describe floating serenely above their bodies and compare the feeling to removing their clothing. In a 2014 study led by Dr. Sam Parnia, author of *What Happens When We Die,* 40 percent of cardiac arrest survivors reported "awareness"—like watching doctors work on their body—while clinically dead.

2. THROUGH THE TUNNEL—A 2001 study from the Netherlands's Hospital Rijnstate found 31 percent of cardiac arrest survivors who had an NDE recalled moving through a tunnel. Anecdotal research shows this can take the form of a cave, kaleidoscope, or valley but is usually cylindrical and delivers the person into an ethereal light. According to Dr. Parnia, this light often leaves people feeling "less materialistic, kinder to others...less afraid of death and generally more pious and religious."

3. VISIONS OF LOVE—After the light, some NDE-ers arrive at heavenly destinations—misty or golden-hued fields, gardens, pathways, and cities of light. Regardless of the geography, survivors report an indescribable feeling of love. A 2017 study from Belgium's University of Liège showed that 80 percent of survivors experienced transcendental peacefulness during their NDE.

4. CLOSE ENCOUNTERS—The University of Liège study also found that 64 percent of participants encountered spirits or people in their NDE. Survivors have recalled meeting deceased loved ones—even pets—as well as spiritual beings, angels, Jesus, God, or a single holy figure of pure light. This being often communicates in an "unspoken language," Dr. Raymond Moody writes.

5. THE LIFE REVIEW—NDE-ers are sometimes presented with a life review—a rapid recall of essential events. These scenes can be shown from another person's perspective, offering insight into past hurts or mistakes. Afterward, Dr. Parnia writes, many survivors "began to view life as an opportunity to be a source of goodness to others."

6. AT THE GATES—By the end of an NDE, most people are directed to return to earth, often to complete their lives and destinies. Most NDE survivors emerge from the experience trans-formed—with, as Dr. Jeffrey Long, author of *God and the Afterlife*, writes, "a profound understanding of God's love."[2]

A number of Christian organizations support the stories of people who have died and seen heaven. Pat Robertson's Christian Broadcasting Network (CBN) airs multiple segments of reenactments of testi-

Most people who've had an out-of-body experience consider it a sacred experience.

monies of people who have seen heaven. Robertson says that a near-death experience puts man face-to-face with God. Evangelical schools such as Liberty University have hosted events featuring the theme that heaven is a real place.

Outside support and reassurance is comforting, but someone who experiences an NDE rarely tries to prove to anyone that the story is true. In fact, most people who've had an out-of-body experience at the time of death consider it a sacred experience and usually have a sense of humility about it. It often takes years before people will share their NDE with anyone except a few close friends or family members.

Comfort in Times of Trouble

As humans, our existence is characterized by pain, sorrow, poverty, persecution, tears, and other troubles. This is the lot of Christians; Jesus warned His disciples, saying, "Blessed are you when others revile you and persecute you and utter all kinds of evil against you falsely on my account. Rejoice and be glad, for your reward is great in heaven, for so they persecuted the prophets who were before you." (Matthew 5:11-12, ESV)

Heaven is where God and His holy angels are, where Jesus is seated on the right hand of God the Father. God is the fountain of love; heaven is filled with God's love. When we die and go to heaven, the pain, sorrow, poverty, persecution, and tears are no more. Instead, we experience an overwhelming divine love in the Father's house.

God Is Love

People from various centuries, cultures, and occupations have documented unique and personal near-death experiences. Yet as we reach back through the centuries of time, most documented stories have one single overwhelming and emotional theme—the realization of God's love.

In March 2003 a little boy nearly four years old lingered between life and death. Colton Burpo underwent surgeries for a ruptured appendix and four abscesses in his abdomen. After the prayers of many people, including his parents, Colton recovered miraculously. Four months later, at age four, Colton told his parents the first of many accounts of what he saw in heaven. Several times Colton emphasized to his parents, "Jesus *really* loves the children."[3]

Records of NDEs show that most people return with what can be described as a divine and even holy comprehension of love, a love they are eager to share and give liberally to people they meet in their everyday lives.

One of the most fascinating accounts of a person's near-death experience was published in the late 1800s, decades before the term NDE was identified. A woman named Rebecca Springer returned from death after an extended illness and wrote of her heavenly experiences in a book originally titled *Intra Muros*.[4] (A later version titled *Within Heaven's Gates* can be found on YouTube, where you can listen to the audiobook in its entirety.)

After she left her body and entered heaven, Rebecca writes, she plunged into the River of Life and experienced healing from all the physical and emotional sorrows from her life on earth. Later, she visited her parents and siblings and extended family. All of them had their own homes built to their particular tastes, and each house structure was built before they arrived. Rebecca's family members enjoyed serving others in heaven as a way of expressing love to the saints and to God. The love was palpable, active, spoken, and pure.

Rebecca and others like her returned from death to tell us one core message: *God is love.*

God's Loving Nature

Love is not merely an attribute of God—it is God's very nature. God is not only loving; He is also fundamentally love. God alone loves in the completeness and perfection of love.

Thus, if God is love and we, His followers, are born of God, then we will also love. God loves us, so we must love one another. A true Christian, one saved by love and filled with God's love, must live in love toward God and others.

The Lord teaches believers how to show His love to others, to our friends, our family, and even our enemies. God's love is unconditional; He loves us simply because He is love.[5]

Rebecca Springer's experience and those of others like her reveal to us that God's love is displayed in the pleasure that He takes in creating a house for each one of us. And what can be better than a home prepared for us by God Himself?

Heaven Is Home

Rebecca Springer wrote about her experience in the antiquated language of a woman who was born in the 1800s. She was escorted from her sickbed and into heaven by her brother-in-law, Frank. As she entered heaven, she asked Frank where they were going.

"Home, little sister," he answered tenderly.

"Home? Have we a home, my brother? Is it anything like these?" I asked, with a wild desire in my heart to cry out for joy.

"Come and see," was his only answer, as he turned into a side path leading toward an exquisitely beautiful house whose columns of very light gray marble shone through the green of the overhanging trees with most inviting beauty.[6]

While we are here on earth, we live in earthly houses, and we live, work, play, talk, and express emotion through our bodies.

Before God created Adam and later Eve, He first created their home, the Garden of Eden. On the sixth and last day of creation, He formed Adam out of the dust of the ground. God also formed the first woman using a rib that He took out of the man—clay formed from clay. "So God created man in his own image, in the image of God created he him; male and female created he them." (Genesis 1:27, KJV) These clay figures were the crescendo of creation! All that God created prior to these clay figures was created *for* these clay figures.

"The Garden of Eden was like heaven on earth," says Jared Wellman, senior pastor at Mission Dorado Baptist Church. Wellman goes on to say, "It existed because God planted it. Although sin didn't yet exist on earth when God originally created the Garden in Eden, it was God's revelation of his beauty, perfection, peace—and really every aspect of his wonderful nature—to mankind. It was where he met with man."[7]

One year after Colton Burpo says he saw heaven, it was Easter time, and his older sister Cassie asked Colton if he knew why Jesus died on the cross. Five-year-old Colton nodded. He said, "Jesus told me He died on the cross so we could go see His dad."[8]

Sometimes a person is told during an NDE that it is not their time. Others who have left their bodies are simply returned.

Now that's the love of God! In simple terms, Colton expressed that our "dad" wants us to come home to see Him!

As Wellman says about heaven, "The Garden that sin destroyed will again be planted, God will again walk with man, and this time there will be no serpent, no forbidden fruit, and no Flood. Just the King and his people."

We wouldn't know about near-death experiences if people who saw heaven didn't return to their earthly body. Accountings of NDEs tell us that sometimes a person is told during an NDE that it is not their time yet. Other times, people who have left their bodies are simply returned. This is what happened to Candy Abbott while undergoing surgery after the birth of her daughter. She was floating down a long hallway filled with peace, love, and serenity. She says she felt like she had come home. Suddenly, though, everything jolted into reverse, and Candy opened her eyes to see a nurse standing over her. Like many who experienced an NDE, Candy knew God was not finished with her—that there was more for her to do.

A Second Chance to Live with Purpose

We often think of the word *ordained* as applying to a person who is officially invested into the ministry or a priestly authority. *Ordained* also means established or ordered by appointment: destined.[9] Each person given the life breath of God has been ordained by God to live a certain timeline of days on earth, and while on earth, we have each been ordained by God to bear fruit that will feed the lives of those with us and then remain here to last after we leave.

> Ye have not chosen me, but I have chosen you, and ordained you, that ye should go and bring forth fruit, and that your fruit should remain. (John 15:16, KJV)

What did Jesus mean when He said, "I have chosen you and appointed you that you should go and bear fruit, and that your fruit should remain"?

Jesus was giving us an analogy to show us that we are here on earth with a divine purpose. An apple tree does not bear apples to have them dangle indefinitely from its sturdy branches. An apple tree bears apples so that fruit can be enjoyed by people. There is fruitfulness and productivity, a gift and calling, given to each of us by God when we are born. God planted those seeds for success inside us at conception, and He delights in watching us grow from infancy to adulthood and every stage in between.

Many people who have witnessed heaven provide overwhelming testimony that they have come back with hope, inspired to live with love, laying their own selfishness aside. NDE-ers say that love is not only realized during the out-of-body experience, but that it also permeates relationships with others after they return. For many, the fear of failure is gone, and a new sense of confidence and purpose arouses them at the dawn of each new day. The promise of life eternal possesses the heart, and a newfound love for God and for all humanity overflows into family, friend, and work relationships. The fear of death is gone.

Many people who have witnessed heaven come back with hope.

There is a realization for some that they've been given a second chance, and they begin to live intentionally, making the most of each opportunity presented and stopping to help someone that they may have previously ignored in their hurry to "do life."

Moses thought about life, death, and our transition to heaven. A few of Moses's thoughts are recorded in the book of Psalms:

> The days of our lives *are* seventy years; And if by reason
> of strength *they are* eighty years. (Psalm 90:10, NKJV)

> So teach *us* to number our days,
> That we may gain a heart of wisdom. (Psalm 90:12, NKJV)

A beautiful thread that is woven into the stories of persons who have experienced death and returned is that they come back to their earthly life with an awareness that God has something for them to do. They realize their days are numbered, and they want to live out their lives with wisdom—concentrating on the work God called them to do rather than personal goals. Moses understood this as well. He finishes off his prayer in Psalm 90 with these words:

> Let Your work appear to Your servants,
> And Your glory to their children.
> And let the beauty of the LORD our God be upon us,
> And establish the work of our hands for us;
> Yes, establish the work of our hands. (Psalm 90:16–17, NKJV)

Moses bemoans the extent of trouble and labor he experienced on earth, yet he also sees that a work ordained by God produces good fruit and radiates the glory of God, even to the next generation of children to see. More than that, Moses sees that the beauty of the Lord rests upon His people and upon the work of their hands. The same Moses who experienced the glory of God in his commission at the burning bush prays that God will establish the work he was doing during his lifetime on earth. The same Moses who met God on Mount Sinai and received the Ten Commandments returned with his countenance shining and a message to deliver to his generation and ours.

A Prayer of Heaven

Dear God,

Thank You for Your promise of heaven, for the beauty, joy, and peace that is Your home.

When my time comes, please see me safely into Your loving arms. Amen.

1 "Dr. Raymond Moody: The Secrets of the Afterlife," Guideposts: Inspirations, September 26, 2016, https://www.guideposts.org/inspiration/life-after-death/dr-raymond-moody-the-secrets-of-the-afterlife.

2 "The Six Stages of a Near-Death Experience," *Mysterious Ways* magazine, https://www.guideposts.org/inspiration/miracles/gods-grace/the-6-stages-of-a-near-death-experience.

3 Todd Burpo with Lynn Vincent, *Heaven Is for Real* (Nashville: Thomas Nelson, 2010), 106.

4 Rebecca Ruter Springer, *Intra Muros* (Elgin, Illinois: A David C. Cook Publication, 1898).

5 Mary Fairchild, "'God Is Love' Bible Verse," Learnreligions.com, accessed June 16, 2020, https://www.learnreligions.com/god-is-love-bible-verse-701340.

6 Rebecca Ruter Springer, *Intra Muros*, 17, 18.

7 "Wellman: Where on Earth Was the Garden of Eden?," January 3, 2015, Odessa American online, https://www.oaoa.com/people/religion/wellman-where-on-earth-was-the-garden-of-eden/article_7d948064-935d-11e4-90c2-4b09cc36f260.html.

8 Todd Burpo with Lynn Vincent, *Heaven Is for Real*, 111.

9 *Merriam-Webster* online, s.v. "ordained," 2020, App.

A Warrior's Vision

By Bud Evans, as told to Ginger Rue

*Let go of all your fears and worries and let God take over.
Giving up control can be difficult but the changes
you see in your life will be worth it.*

Lisa Rusczyk, EdD

Evans, we got you! It's going to be all right! You need to stay with us!"

I held on to the medic, pleading with him, "I don't want to go! You guys gotta keep me. You gotta save me!" I can still remember all of it so clearly: the smell of my skin burning, my sergeant using his knife to try to pick the pieces of scalding metal off my flesh, the medic holding my hand as I screamed.

The date was June 24, 2004, and I was nineteen years old. In fact, it was the day before my twentieth birthday. My infantry unit had been doing a night patrol on the outskirts of Hawija, Iraq.

There were five of us in the alpha team, all men: Sergeant Waters, our squad leader; Private Perales; Private Helon; Staff Sergeant Gregory; and me. My job was SAW gunner. SAW stands for "squad automatic weapon," a machine gun that shoots hundreds of rounds a minute and is the largest machine gun that soldiers are allowed to take into buildings.

I was stationed on the roof of the Humvee with my SAW. I thought my biggest challenge of the night would be just not falling off the roof as we traveled along the bumpy roads. It had been a quiet night, and we were on our way back to base. We had no idea we were walking into an ambush.

Bullets were flying everywhere. We were pinned down.

Suddenly a rocket appeared overhead. I could hardly believe what I was seeing: it was like watching death coming right at me—coming so fast that there was no time to move. The rocket drifted slightly to the left and then to the right in a sweeping motion.

"We've got contact to the right!" I yelled. Just then the enemy started shooting at us from behind a huge fallen tree and a stack of old bricks. I grabbed my SAW, jumped off the truck, and ran. I saw a pile of bricks next to a generator used for pumping water out of a well. I ran behind it, all the while engaging the enemy as I moved. Once I had cover, I tried to put down cover fire so that the rest of my team could push forward. Bullets were flying everywhere. We were pinned down.

We radioed our squad's bravo team, as well as another squad that was out in another part of the city. If they could arrive in time, that would give us a total of three teams to return fire. That's the kind of fighting odds the military likes: outgunning the enemy three to one. But with the other teams on the opposite side of the city, for now, it was just the five of us holding our position and biding our time. We would have to maintain fire superiority over the enemy until the other teams could get there to flank and neutralize the target.

"Talk the rifles!" Sergeant Waters yelled.

In combat, the military uses a tactic called "talking the rifles" whereby soldiers use suppressive fire to pin down the enemy. The main goal of this system is not necessarily to hit the enemy, but to suppress the enemy soldiers' fire—to shoot constantly so they're forced to keep their heads down. Talking the rifles is basically taking turns shooting. The first man shoots four times: *pop pop pop pop*. Then the second man: *pop pop pop pop*. Then the third, then the fourth. I was number four.

Talking the rifles, ideally, gives each soldier on the team time to reload. Ideally. But for whatever reason during that firefight, two soldiers had to reload at once. That meant I had to shoot longer, and since my shots were all coming from the same location, the enemy must have had time to peek out from their cover. And in the darkness, they could see the muzzle blast. They knew right where I was. That's when they shot a rocket right at me.

It didn't hit me, but it was fairly close. When the rocket hit the ground and exploded, shrapnel ricocheted off the bricks, piercing my left side. Since I'm left-handed, my left arm was up, exposing the soft shell under my arm where the vest wasn't plated with metal. The impact of the explosion threw me. I flew backward about four or five feet, my SAW going another three feet or so.

I remember lying on the ground for a moment, then suddenly being filled with rage. I opened my armored vest, put my hand on my ribs, and then pulled my hand back out. Even in the darkness, I could see and feel that it was covered in blood. I could feel adrenaline flooding my body, and I was furious.

At that point, the thought of dying hadn't even entered my mind. I just wanted revenge so badly that I couldn't even think straight. I stood up to reengage the enemy, completely forgetting that I had been blown away from my cover. I felt myself get hit in the side, where I'd been hit just moments before by shrapnel. That was when the pain started. I couldn't breathe. No matter how hard I tried to take in air, I couldn't get a breath. Each time I tried to breathe, it felt like someone was squeezing my lungs tighter and tighter. I remember thinking, *Oh no! I'm going to die!*

I fell to the ground, and the pain began setting in even more. I lay there, fighting for air, until Perales grabbed me and started dragging my body back to cover with the rest of the team. I could feel something coming from my lungs, out of my mouth and nose. It was my own blood, and I was choking on it. I tried to cough up the blood so that I could take in some air, but I guess I couldn't get enough pressure behind my lungs to push the blood out. I knew I needed to take a breath, and I knew I needed to blow the blood out of my mouth, but I couldn't do either.

I heard Sergeant Waters saying, "Go on, Bud. We got you. It's going to be all right. We're going to get you taken care of." But I could see from the look on his face that he wasn't so sure. That's when I started going under.

Surviving Childhood

Fear wasn't something I struggled with when I joined the military. The way I looked at it, after surviving the first nine years of my childhood in Las Vegas, I could survive anything.

My younger brother, John, and I grew up in an abusive household. Our biological father, whom I call Lloyd to this day when I speak of him because I refuse to call him Dad, was an alcoholic who was always angry—not just at John, my mom, and me, but at anybody who crossed his path. In addition to beating us with his fists, a belt, or a wrench—or anything else he could use to hurt us—he also liked to mess with our heads and make us feel like we were less than nothing.

If I could survive the first nine years of my childhood, I could survive anything.

John and I learned early on to look out for each other. At that time we couldn't count on our mom because she worked full time and was using drugs—mostly cocaine, speed, and crystal meth, but also some marijuana and alcohol. When she was around, she was often the punching bag. I remember seeing Lloyd grab her by the throat and pin her against the wall as he punched her in the face. Then he'd punch the wall beside her head and tell her that he didn't hit her the second time because he loved her so much—like she should be grateful. It seemed there was no one who could stand up to a monster as big and mean as Lloyd.

Once, when I was seven years old, Lloyd came after me with so much rage. Our little dog named Smith, a shepherd/border collie mix, tried to save me—she jumped up and bit Lloyd on the arm. Lloyd turned to Smith and started beating her, screaming that he was going to kill my dog. I snapped! I kicked Lloyd in the groin as hard as I could. When he dropped Smith, she and I ran for our lives.

I came back home later that night, after Mom was home from work. Lloyd was passed out by then. The next day, he acted as though nothing had ever happened. This was the pattern: Lloyd would get drunk or high and then abuse me, my brother, and my mom. Then he'd pretend nothing had ever happened.

John and I learned early on to look out for each other.

Eventually, my mom divorced Lloyd and married a man who lived across the street from us. His name was Don. At first, I was angry about the whole thing; anger had become my default emotion. I suppose I had picked it up from Lloyd. When Don and my mom told John and me that they were getting married and we were all going to live together, I bolted from their embrace and took off running down the street. Don came chasing after me, following me for a few blocks until he caught up.

"Look," Don said. "Things are going to get better. School's going to get better. Life's going to get better." I wanted to believe him, but I didn't know how. As the two of us walked back toward home together, we were suddenly surrounded by five members of a well-known gang from our neighborhood. Rough guys.

Don got behind me and put one hand over my chest and the other over my head, attempting to shield me. The gang members started saying things about how Lloyd had put them up to getting his revenge on Don. Lloyd couldn't stand to see my mom happy; he wanted her to suffer.

As the gang members drew closer to us, Don whispered to me, "When I tell you, run and don't look back. Tell your mom to call the police. Don't look back; just go." Another gang member joined the others. This one had a baseball bat. When he ran up and hit Don on the head with the bat, Don shouted, "Now!"

I ran as fast as I could for the house, but although Don had told me not to, I couldn't help but look back. He was lying on the ground, and the gang members were kicking him and stomping on his head. Mom had come looking for us and had seen the gang approach, so she'd already called the police.

Don wound up in the hospital for some time. I thought he might decide that Mom, John, and I were more trouble than we were worth, but he stuck by us. My grandparents (my mom's parents) were always so loving to John and me and had always tried to help us in any way they could. They paid to fly John and me to Minnesota for a couple of months to live with my aunt until Don recovered and he and Mom could get everything together for us to all move to Indiana, far away from Lloyd. She never could've done it if it hadn't been for financial support from her mom and stepdad. Their only request was to get me and John in church as soon as we got settled. Mom and Don agreed.

Surprisingly, Lloyd fought my mother for custody. I don't think it was because he actually wanted John and me; I think he just wanted to spite Mom and Don. I remember telling John that I would stay with Lloyd.

Maybe if I stay, he won't chase us all down and try to find us, I reasoned. Part of me thought it was my job as the older brother to protect John, even if it meant sacrificing myself. Maybe another part of me thought I could somehow change Lloyd. Truthfully, I desperately wanted him to love me. I wanted a loving father like the dads I saw on TV. I wanted to hear my dad say, "I'm proud of you" or "You did well."

Thankfully, the court system saw the situation more clearly than I did as a nine-year-old kid, because they awarded custody to my mom. I can see now that there was nothing I could have done to make Lloyd the father I needed him to be. He just didn't have it in him.

But Don did.

A New Beginning

When we got settled in Indiana, Don gathered us all for a family meeting. He looked at us with a great tenderness in his eyes and promised, "No one will ever hurt any of you again. No one will ever put hands on you again. Nor will I put my hands on any of you." Don didn't want us living in the shadow of Lloyd's abuse anymore. He understood that the scars of abuse are more than just physical, so he told us he'd arranged for John and me to begin therapy so that we could recover emotionally. The way he saw it, we all had a part to play in getting better.

I grew to trust Don and rely on him, just like the boys on TV did with their dads.

For her part, Mom had fought valiantly to get off drugs before we moved from Vegas. She and Don promised us a new beginning and a better life. I didn't say anything during this meeting, but in my head, I remember thinking, *I'll believe it when I see it.*

And see it, I did. From the get-go, I saw Don make sacrifices for us. He worked hard and spent money wisely. We didn't have a lot of money, but I remember that he bought John and me both a nice bed of our own; eventually, we moved from a trailer to a house where we each had our own bedroom. This was huge because all our lives, John and I had always had to share not only a room but also a bed. When we thanked him, Don simply said, "I'm always going to do whatever I can to make it better for you guys."

He meant it too. Don went out of his way for us in every area. For example, he himself never had a nice car. He drove junky vehicles all the time and was always having to do some sort of maintenance on them. But he made sure that Mom always had a good, reliable vehicle and that John and I did, too, when we were old enough to drive. I grew to trust Don and rely on him, just like boys on TV did with their dads.

Even so, John and I had scars from our upbringing with Lloyd. We both dealt with anger and lashed out inappropriately at times. I remember once when we'd done something bad, another adult said something to Don in front of us. "You need to correct those kids with some physical punishment," the man said. I could feel my whole body tense up and I got scared. I wondered if Don was going to start beating us the way Lloyd had.

Don took a deep breath and replied to the person who offered the advice. "Those kids have been hit enough," he said firmly. "They don't need any more of that. And it will never happen again as long as I'm around."

I remember relief washing over me. Of course John and I weren't perfect, but Don still loved us. He'd often tell us how proud of us he was, even though I couldn't think of any reason he should be. "What are you proud of us for?" I would ask. I had severe learning disabilities and never did so hot in school, so it wasn't like I was making the honor roll. But Don would find something to praise in me. "You're completing your counseling" or "You're going to therapy and working hard there" or whatever. It just felt nice. It was such a great feeling to know he was always behind me, always there for me.

I decided to believe in God for one reason: because you can't hate someone you don't believe in.

Mom worked until six o'clock every night, and Don, a trucker, had to travel a lot, so John and I vacuumed, washed dishes, and took out the trash. We kept the yard up. No one told us we had to do chores; we just did them. John and I wanted Don to stick around—we didn't want to be the reason he left. Once, I did something wrong and didn't tell Don, and when he found out, he told me he was disappointed in me. That hurt me worse than any beating I ever got from Lloyd. I was so afraid that I'd now given Don a reason to leave. I didn't understand then that it wouldn't have mattered what I did—Don would never have abandoned us.

Learning about God

My parents had promised my grandparents that our family would find a church and worship regularly, and they intended to keep that promise. Both Don and my mom had been brought up in church as kids but had, like so many people, gotten caught up in the stereotypical, wild Vegas lifestyle. But I suppose they felt that they'd walked around lost long enough, because once we started going to church, neither of them ever looked back.

I'd never been to church before, but I could sense that the congregation Don and Mom had chosen—a small country church of about forty-five people—was a place of authenticity. The members were extremely earnest in their faith and devoted themselves wholeheartedly to the work of the church. We went every Sunday. Mom and Don got involved in the congregation's ministries and tried to keep John and me excited about going.

I paid careful attention to the lessons from the pulpit and in Sunday school, especially the ones about how great God is and about how He controls everything—how He'd set the whole world in motion and how nothing happened without His permission. How He is our heavenly Father. But rather than giving me a sense of peace, the whole idea absolutely enraged me. If all this were true, then what had happened to me throughout my life hadn't been Lloyd's fault. It had been God's fault! At least, that was how my mind reasoned as a child.

I decided to believe in God for one reason only: because you can't hate someone you don't believe in. We studied the book of Job intensely in Sunday school, and I couldn't believe how God was messing with this poor guy's life. Why did He let all these things happen to Job? Why didn't He tell the devil to stop? I saw God as a powerful brute who played with human beings as a game. I hated Him for having sat there in His golden chair while my mom, my brother, and I had suffered from Lloyd's abuse.

I kept my thoughts to myself so as not to upset Mom and Don, but I dedicated myself to learning all I could about God. I suppose that, even as a kid, I had a soldier's mindset: know your enemy. I would pray, almost daring God to give me one little sign, something to prove that He really was so great and powerful like people at church said. But when no sign came, I took it as proof that I was right: either God wasn't really so powerful, or He just didn't care.

An Earthly Father

Meanwhile, our family of four grew closer and closer. Don's gentle, dependable ways helped me grow to trust and rely on him.

After we'd been living in Indiana for a couple of years, when I was about eleven, I remember talking with Mom one day before Don came home from work. I asked, "Do you think Don would be upset if we called...if I called him 'Dad'?"

As I grew older, I could ever so slightly feel my attitude toward God begin to soften.

"No," Mom replied. "I don't think he'd be upset at all. In fact, I think that's something he's been waiting for, for a long time. But he didn't want to push that on you boys. He didn't want you to feel like you had to."

That weekend, when I was helping Don change the brakes on his car, I decided to ask him the big question. I was so scared. What if he said no? What if I created an awkwardness and ruined everything? I was afraid to open up my heart because if it didn't happen, I'd kick myself for hoping. Finally, I mustered the courage and spit it out.

"Don," I said. "Would it be okay with you if I started calling you 'Dad' from now on?"

A huge grin spread across his face. "Yeah, obviously!" Don enveloped me in a hug. "I've waited a long time to hear that, son."

Before Don, my concept of a father was someone who was vindictive and mean. No wonder my first instinct toward God, who I was told was my heavenly Father, was anger. I didn't really understand what it meant when I'd hear people pray using the words "heavenly Father." The term *father* had never meant unconditional love, acceptance, and respect. But because of Don, I was rethinking everything I thought I understood about how fathers care for their children.

Maybe it was Don showing me what a true father looks like, or maybe it was the counseling, or maybe the regular church attendance, or a combination of all three, but as I grew older, I could ever so slightly feel my attitude toward God begin to soften.

Finding Faith

When I was thirteen, our Sunday school teacher suggested that Mom sign John and me up for church camp that summer. My teacher knew we didn't have a lot of extra money, so she had arranged for the church to cover our fee. I'd heard of other kids going to summer camp, but since it had never been something we could afford, I'd never even hoped for such an opportunity.

When Mom and Don said we could go, I was pretty excited about the prospect of all that outdoor fun. I knew that since it was church camp, they'd try to sneak in some religion, but I decided ahead of time that I wasn't going to fall for any of that. I was going in hard, and they weren't going to get me!

As much as I tried to focus only on the swimming and hiking and games, though, when it came time for praise and worship, I couldn't deny that I was witnessing something extraordinary. It was like I could feel the Holy Spirit filling the room, touching the hearts of the souls gathered together.

It sounds beautiful, but for me, it wasn't a good feeling. Far from it.

Hebrews 4:12 (ESV) says that the Word of God is "sharper than any two-edged sword, piercing to the division of soul and of spirit, of joints and of marrow, and discerning the thoughts and intentions of the heart." That was exactly what it felt like to me—like I was being stabbed. The message seemed to point directly to me. Instead of making me repentant, it made me angry and aggressive.

"I do want Jesus in my life," I said as I choked back tears. "But does Jesus want me?"

After about the sixth night of worship, I decided I couldn't sit through it anymore. I got up and walked out. I was furious and felt like I just wanted to punch somebody. The speaker had said that God allowed things to happen in our lives not because of malice, but because they were supposed to be opportunities to let Him lead us. When he said that, all I could think of was my childhood with Lloyd. Was that supposed to be God's idea of leading? If so, it seemed pretty messed up to me. I wanted to scream, "I will not accept God's leadership!" So I stormed out before I lost it in front of everyone.

A camp counselor followed me outside and asked what was wrong. I cried bitter, angry tears.

"Where has He been?" I demanded. "He's supposed to be leading me? Well, I never saw Him! Where was He when all these things happened to me?"

The counselor put his hand on my shoulder. "Bud," he said gently. "He's been right beside you the whole time. You just never opened your heart to see it." He asked me if I wanted to make a change. "Do you want Jesus in your life?"

I'd promised myself I wouldn't let them get to me, and inside, I berated myself for being weak. The anger in my heart had become a familiar companion by this point in my life. I didn't know how to live without it; it was as though it fueled everything I did. But the burden of it was so heavy. I longed to let it go, to walk free of it, yet the prospect was terrifying. I choked back tears. "I do want Jesus in my life," I said. "But does Jesus want me?"

The camp counselor and I argued back and forth for nearly an hour about whether I was good enough for God and whether God was good enough for me. Whenever I felt like I was about to give in, I kept trying to justify why I didn't need Jesus in my life.

"Bud, I know you're angry," the counselor finally said. "But when you were a little boy and you were crying and suffering, Jesus was crying and suffering with you the whole time."

That broke me. I couldn't stop bawling. I felt like I was being weak for accepting Jesus, but at the same time, the thought of letting go of my anger and bitterness filled me with overwhelming relief. The counselor and I walked back into the big room and went up to the front. I looked out over the crowd of about two hundred people and confessed that I believed that Jesus was the Son of God and that I wanted Him to be Lord of my life.

I wanted to be baptized, but I decided to wait until I went back home so that Mom and Don could be there for it. I thought after the confession that I'd go back to my seat, but I couldn't—I was practically mobbed. It seemed that every one of those two hundred people crowded around me and hugged me and prayed for me. The camp counselor smiled and said, "See? You're not alone."

Back at home, I confessed Jesus again before our church congregation, and we all went down to a nearby creek, where I was baptized.

The camp counselor had warned me that it would be easy to follow Jesus at church camp but harder when I went back to "real life." He was right. Lloyd still took up a lot of real estate in my head, and to this day, he still does. I've come to learn that abuse lingers in the recesses of the human mind that way. But I could see the Spirit working in my life, helping me in my understanding and growing my faith. I thought more and more about what we'd studied in Sunday school about Job.

I could see the Spirit working in my life, helping me in my understanding and growing my faith.

For years, I'd struggled with that story. Whenever the preacher would talk about "God's timing" and how God wasn't bound by human constraints of time and how He did things according to His own purpose when it was the right time to do them, I'd always think it was just a big cop-out. I'd always want to scream, "What would you know? Did you ever sit there and feel that buckle wrap around your back or smack you in the skull? Why wasn't that the right time for God to intervene?"

For a long time, I'd thought that Don had saved us by getting us out of Las Vegas and away from Lloyd. But then I started to realize that maybe it was God who had sent Don to do that.

I started to see that what happened to Job wasn't some bet that God had made. God knew Job. He knew that Job was strong enough to withstand that pressure without renouncing Him. And while I don't think God "picked" me for the abuse I endured, I think He knew that I had the potential to grow up to become the adult who would find Him and break that cycle that had begun when Lloyd himself was abused as a child.

I started to think maybe that was what people meant when they talked about things happening in God's timing. It was about recognizing our time to be called to do God's work. I realized that God had, indeed, rescued us through Don and that I had free will so that I could choose who I became. Lloyd had chosen to follow the path of an abuser, but that didn't mean I had to do the same.

A Godly Influence

I'd come to Indiana an angry kid who fought against God, and then I became a Christian. I'd also come to Indiana as a kid who hated school, but I suppose God wanted to change that too. I believe He sent a special teacher into my life for that purpose.

My teachers in Las Vegas had always been mean. They'd never tried to hide their complete disdain for me. It was as though they took my learning disabilities as a personal affront or as proof that I wasn't worthy of instruction. One of them had even told my mom that I was just a bad kid and there was no hope for me and that I didn't deserve to get to go to school. Mom had wanted to go to the principal to complain, but she'd figured that the word of a drug-addict mom wouldn't get very far against the word of a teacher. I'd learned to just take whatever my teachers in Vegas dished out, so it is no surprise that I hated school.

In my high school in Indiana, I was assigned to Mrs. Marlow. She was the special-education teacher for kids who had learning disabilities in math and English. She was different from any teacher I'd ever had before. She radiated joy and offered love and acceptance to everyone. She made me believe she was actually happy to see me every day. She made me believe I could learn. Even though she was assigned to me just for math and English, she always took the time to help me with any other classes when I needed her.

I think Mrs. Marlow's loving spirit was the kind that can come only from joy in the Lord. Mrs. Marlow's husband was a preacher, and she lived her faith genuinely and whole-heartedly for all to see. She would always attend student-led prayer gatherings at the flagpole before school, and she sponsored Christian clubs. She paid real attention to how we were doing, and if she saw kids who were struggling with something, she'd stop them in the hallways to pray for them, right then and there.

> *I think Mrs. Marlow's loving spirit was the kind that can come only from joy in the Lord.*

Mrs. Marlow didn't just believe in me: she *actively* believed in me. If I didn't do my best, she'd tell me, "Bud, you sold yourself short. You have so much more to offer." No other teacher had ever made me feel worthwhile before. I couldn't help but look up to Mrs. Marlow, and my whole family had so much respect for her that we even attended her church for a while.

Having a teacher tell me that I could achieve anything meant so much to me. Mom and Don had always encouraged me, but I cherished that validation from such a smart lady who didn't owe me a thing. Mrs. Marlow had taught thousands of students, so she knew what she was talking about, I reasoned. If she said I could do it, I could do it. All those teachers in Las Vegas who said I was a lost cause who would never graduate from high school? They'd all been wrong.

A Soldier's Life

After high school graduation, I decided to join the military. I knew it wouldn't be as easy as just signing up, though. Even though I'd made a lot of progress in my emotional and spiritual development, I still had a lot of anger inside me. I hadn't really taken charge of my life fully, but I wanted to make a change and make a difference in the world. Lloyd had tried to make me believe I was nothing, but I didn't want to be nothing.

I was overweight and was told I had to lose thirty pounds before the army would take me. I'd also have to pass a test, which scared me given my track record in school. But I remembered a wise saying I'd heard before. Maybe Mom had said it or maybe it was Mrs. Marlow; I couldn't remember where I'd heard it exactly, but the words resonated clearly: "Don't sit and wish; stand and do." It was time to make something happen, so I got to work. I told myself if I could make it through nine years with Lloyd, I could do anything.

I studied hard, passed the test, and lost those thirty pounds. I realized that God hadn't taken that test for me or magically caused me to lose weight, but I hadn't done it on my own either. He'd given me the patience and the ability to do it. I felt like God was on my side, and so were my parents and my brother, and even Mrs. Marlow.

My decision to stop making excuses and start getting things done was exactly in line with the military's philosophy. During my fourteen weeks of basic training at Fort Benning in Georgia, I lost another thirty-five pounds quickly. One thing I loved about the army was that it gave me a lot of positive reinforcement on a daily basis. If you kept your area clean or put in extra work, your superior would praise you, often to the whole barracks. I was watched even when I didn't know I was being watched, and my drill sergeant would call me into his office and commend me for a job well done. After all those years as a little boy starved for a father's approval, I ate it up.

For the first time in my life, I felt like I was really and truly good at something. I got better at the things I wasn't good at. It's never fun to be corrected. No soldier wants to have to do push-ups until he cries and then have to roll over and do sit-ups and then run laps, but the thing about these corrective actions is that someone is putting in the time to rebuild you instead of just saying, "Get out; you're not worth it." The army was making an investment in me, molding me into someone of value to them. For me, being part of the army was easier than going to school had been. They laid everything out for me: "This is what we're doing, how we're doing it, and where it's going." There was always the assumption that I was capable, no matter how difficult the task seemed at first try.

For instance, I was horrible at shooting when we first started, but I followed directions and kept trying until eventually I qualified as expert with my rifle. When I became a sergeant, I was in the position to praise other soldiers. It was a neat feeling to know that some of the troops wondered, *What does Sergeant Evans think about me?* But one thing I knew was that I'd never mistreat anyone under me. I chose to be a Don instead of a Lloyd, a Mrs. Marlow instead of one of my Las Vegas teachers. I gave my trainees the same positive reinforcement that had meant so much to me. As far as I'm concerned, a good soldier is built on one thing, and that's believing he's a good soldier.

Although I loved military life, it didn't leave a lot of time for me to study my Bible and think about God, especially since I'd chosen the infantry track. But it was almost impossible not to think about God when I was deployed to Iraq

It was almost impossible not to think about God when I was deployed to Iraq.

less than a year after I'd completed training. After a big firefight or an IED (improvised explosion device) blast, a lot of times the other soldiers would say, "Man, we were lucky," and I'd think, *Were we lucky, or was it God's saving grace?* There's a saying that there are no atheists in foxholes, and I saw that firsthand. Even the biggest nonbelievers, when they got hurt, would all of a sudden start asking, "Do you think I'll go to heaven?"

Once a guy said to me, "Bud, I know that you believe in God. What's going to happen to me?"

I told him, "You're going to live—that's what's going to happen to you." As for me, I felt like my time would come when it came, but until then, God had a plan for me.

I guess the biggest thing I learned from being in the army was sheer fortitude. Whenever I thought something was too hard, I made myself rethink and say, "No, it's too easy." In a moment when you think it's too hard, you've already given up. And I couldn't afford to give up because it wasn't all about me.

The military is a team. If I failed, I risked hurting someone else; if someone else failed, they risked putting me in danger. There's no room in the army for a "whatever" attitude—it's all about responsibility. Whenever I felt that I couldn't make it through Iraq, I just reminded myself that after all I had gone through with Lloyd, anything had to be achievable and doable.

As a result of that mindset, I worked hard at everything I did. If I picked up trash, I strove to be the best at trash pickup. If I did push-ups, I strove to be the best at push-ups. At nineteen years old, I was at the top of my game in terms of both my physical strength and my mental determination and still climbing. The army helped me see the bigger picture and helped me understand more about God's timing. That helped me find a measure of peace in my life.

> *The army helped me see the bigger picture and helped me understand more about God's timing.*

But deep inside, the anger I'd relied on to get me through my childhood trauma was still there. I suppose God had a plan to put even that anger to use, because when I was hit in Hawija, it fueled my initial determination to survive.

The Heat of Battle

Sergeant Waters held on to me and kept telling me it was going to be all right. Good old Waters—H20, as we called him. I knew him well enough to know that he was as scared as I was. Before Iraq, when we'd been stationed in Hawaii, we'd barbecue together and have parties.

"Evans, it's going to be all right," he kept saying. "We got you, man. We got you." I could tell, though, from the look on his face that the damage was worse than what I'd thought. Still, I didn't think about dying. I really didn't. When you feel unstoppable, dying just doesn't seem like an option. How could I possibly be in danger of dying? I had the best materials a soldier could have at that time: body armor, flak jacket, night-vision goggles with infrared lasers, a scope on my rifle, and my SAW. Not to mention that we all had first-aid pouches and were trained how to use them.

Waters spoke tersely into the radio: "We need bravo team here!" Bravo had our medic. "We need Doc here because Evans is shot!" Waters yelled into the radio. Then he turned to me again. "I got you, man; it's going to be all right." But I knew he was lying. I could feel his fear like a hollow pit inside my gut.

I also felt my side burning from the sharp metal imbedded in my flesh. "Get that stuff out of my side," I said to Waters. He started trying to pick it out, and I could smell the wound burning. Meanwhile, the other guys were still laying down suppressive fire.

I remember thinking, *Wow, this is just like the movies*. I took one more look at Waters's worried face before I lost consciousness.

The Vision

The next thing I knew, it was like I was in the bottom of a pool. I wasn't choking anymore, but I wasn't holding my breath either. I could breathe freely in this pool. I wasn't drowning. I realized that this was possible because I wasn't in that wounded body anymore; I was outside it.

But I wasn't afraid. I felt complete peace. All fear of choking and drowning was gone, and I could open my eyes. I've never been able to open my eyes while swimming, but here it didn't bother me at all. And this place wasn't like any swimming pool I'd ever seen. This was more like a giant, clear cylinder, like a glass or a cup, and there was no way to actually swim around. I was flanked on both sides of the glass by images.

I looked around me and saw scenes from my life, even scenes I wouldn't have been able to remember, like my mother giving birth to me in the delivery room. On one side, I saw a scene from my life, and on the other side, across from it, was what I would describe as alternative scenarios to each scene. It was as though one side was the life I'd actually lived and the other side showed various options for the life that I could have had. I couldn't interact with these scenes, just view them. There was no one to guide me, but I had the ability to swim upward to see more options. I remember going through it all and just taking it in.

I looked around and saw scenes from my life, even scenes I wouldn't have been able to remember.

As I swam upward, the scenes from my life, and the alternate versions of those scenes, went up in a chronological order as well. On one side was my childhood with Lloyd, and on the other side were the other ways it could have gone. One scene was if Mom hadn't ever married Lloyd; another was if I hadn't been born; another was if I'd been born to someone else; and still another was if I'd been given up for adoption. I even witnessed a scene in which my younger brother,

John, was older than I was and I was born a girl, giving him a sister instead of a brother. All the options for my life I'd ever wondered about were presented before me, but not as if I were looking at framed television screens; it wasn't that simple. When I turned my head to one side, I viewed my whole life in three-dimensional form. The farther up I swam, the older I was in the images. It was like swimming through my life from the very beginning.

Throughout the vision, I kept seeing things that happened as well as things that had not. Some of the scenes I saw—the ones that I had not actually lived—made me wish for the alternate version. For example, I saw scenes from my school years. There was the version I had actually lived, with teachers yelling at me and telling me I was a horrible student who would never make it, and then there was a version where I was a good student and things came easily to me. So many true scenes from my childhood hurt me to look at, and I wondered why those things had happened to me. It was terrifying to see Lloyd again, exactly the way I remembered him. He was just as scary as the day we left. I could see my own body, nearly twenty years old, taking in this vision, but I still felt the same fear I felt as a small child.

Alternate scenes of my having a childhood without Lloyd were almost as unbearable because I felt jealous of the "me" who could have had such a good life. But just as I started to feel the familiar anger I always carried well up inside me, a peace I'd never felt before washed over me. I felt like God was showing me what He'd been trying to teach me over the past few years about time and how He exists outside our human concept of it—as though He was reminding me that I had lived through a sad chapter in my life that He had closed in

His time. Still, it was a chapter I didn't want to revisit. *I don't want to see this*, I thought. *I don't want that.* And so I looked away to a different part of my life where Lloyd was no longer there.

During this whole time of seeing these visions, I never once thought about the fact that I'd been shot and was waiting for help to arrive. I wasn't on the battlefield anymore. I was here, in this cylindrical pool that showed me what my life had been and what it could have been. I felt no pain from my injury. All I could focus on was this opportunity I'd been given to see these visions. All the events in my life, even the moments I'd tried so desperately to forget, were replayed before me. I had no concept of how long it was taking to relive every memory of my whole life, plus looking at the various scenarios of how each moment could have gone. During this vision, I existed outside time. There was no rush.

Gradually, I made it to my more recent past. I saw myself swearing my oath to the US military. I saw myself doing well in my training. It wasn't like just watching a movie of my life. When I looked at those happy images, I felt in my core the exact same feelings I'd felt in all those moments, with the same intensity, like they were all happening right then. I saw moments of my life that had not happened...yet. What did this mean? Was God showing me what would happen to me if I lived? Or was it just a hope of a life that was never to be?

At just shy of twenty years old, the thought of having a family had always seemed like something far in the future. Even though I was so young and so devoted to being a soldier, I suppose I always carried a hope that one day I'd be a husband and father and I'd love my family well in spite of the horrible example Lloyd had set for me.

And yet the prospect of my own loving family seemed almost a pipe dream: I knew that abuse was a cycle that generally perpetuated itself by damaging the children to the point that they grew up to be just like their abusive parents. But here, as I swam upward in this cylinder, I saw myself with a family of my own—not a dysfunctional family, but a good, stable one.

To get there, I had to swim past the vision of myself being shot. Because I could see the future just ahead, I swam past the vision of myself lying on the ground with the medic working on me. I had no time to dwell on that. I could see myself just ahead with my own family, and I longed to see who they were.

When I reached the vision of my future family, I couldn't see faces. None of it had happened in my physical life's timeline, so I suppose the picture of their faces was not yet to be revealed to me. But in spite of not seeing their faces, I could intensely feel every emotion the future "me" in the visions felt. The woman in the vision said, "Babe, I love you," and I felt the warmth of that to my very core. She never explained, "I'm your wife," but I knew by the way she spoke to me who she was. I could feel that reassurance that she would always be there.

I saw moments of my life that had not happened...yet. Was God showing me what would happen to me if I lived?

Then I heard two children's voices saying, "We love you, Dad." One voice was a boy; the other, a girl. The image was so dark that I couldn't see anyone clearly, but in spite of that darkness, nothing about it was scary. All I felt was peace. At one point, I remember saying to myself, *Oh man. I want this. This was meant to be.*

I'd always thought I'd found my place in life when I joined the military. I loved the army; I loved the infantry. But this feeling I got from hearing this future family tell me they loved me? It was like nothing I'd ever experienced before. Simple words uttered by people I hadn't even met yet, but I could feel that love, and I realized, *This is what I want. I want to have this.*

I think God knows exactly what each of us needs in every moment.

I've heard stories that some people who die and are revived, or who nearly die, have seen the gates of heaven, but I think God knows exactly what each of us needs in every moment. And for me, seeing and hearing that family of my own, feeling their love so completely, was everything I wanted and needed. It was my heaven. God knows me well enough that He knew exactly what it would take to make me fight for my life.

Instantly, upon having that realization, it was like the click of a door closing. I knew that being outside my body meant that I would not live to see the future that had been shown to me, that if I wanted this future, I had to get back into my body. And to get back into my body, I had to swim to the top of that cylinder. I had to get back to the battlefield if I wanted this vision of my future life to actually come to pass. I had to get my head above water if I wanted to live.

So it was fear that made me swim, fear of losing what I'd been shown. I swam with everything I had, and I remember feeling myself getting closer and closer to the surface. I felt strong and excited that I was getting there. Then I could feel my lungs compressing. I had been under too long. I wouldn't make it. I swam harder and harder, but it became more and more difficult. Yet I was so close!

Suddenly my elbow broke the surface of the water. Then my hand, my forearm reached past the water line. But then I began sinking. No, no, no! I fought harder and harder. If I didn't get my head above water and take a breath, I knew I would die. And if I died, the future family I had seen would never happen. I became angry with God. Why would He taunt me like this, dangling the thing I most wanted in front of my eyes, only to pull it away?

In that moment, I was scared of dying. I hadn't felt afraid of dying when I'd gotten shot, but now I realized that dying meant never getting the things I now knew I truly wanted in life. I could feel my future wife and my children's confidence in me, their love. I didn't want to let them down.

As I continued to sink, I returned to the point in the visions where I felt my future family's presence. I still couldn't see their faces, but I could feel their love. I could feel them hugging and kissing me. I could feel everything I was going to lose, but no matter how hard I tried, I didn't have the strength to swim up again. I had to accept the fact that I couldn't swim anymore, that I would die. But I wanted my last moment to be the one with my wife and children. That was how I wanted to go. Before I would have to release it forever, I tried to take in every bit of this feeling I would never have. I was going to die, and there was nothing I could do.

Then, the water was gone. It was as though the pool had been suddenly drained.

Back in the Fight

Evans, you need to stay with us!"

Bravo team had made it to our location. Doc was draining my lung to clear the blood out. I held on to him and pleaded, "I don't want to die! I don't want to go! You guys gotta keep me! You gotta save me!"

"Yeah, man, we got you," Doc said. But I was still so scared. And once again, angry. Not angry about my past like I had always been, but angry about losing the future I would never have. I wanted to fight for it. I didn't know how old I was in the vision where I had my own family, but I knew that I wanted to live to experience it, however long it took to come. I didn't know how I would even meet my wife. All I knew was that I'd been given the opportunity to see something that I could have in my life, and I wanted to make it happen.

Meanwhile, the rest of the troops were still engaging the enemy. They called in a Black Hawk helicopter to get me out of there. They put me on a gurney, but with all the engagement from the enemy, the helicopter crew didn't know where they could land in order to pick me up. When they were finally able to land, they told me to lie down and rest, but I didn't want to.

> *I didn't know how old I was in the vision, but I knew that I wanted to live to experience it.*

"Look, this is my first time on a helicopter," I said. "I want to see the takeoff."

"Sure, sure," the helicopter medic said. Then he injected me with something. I thought he was giving me some IV fluids, but it was actually morphine. I began feeling sleepy. I remember telling him, "I'm just going to lie down for a quick second if that's all right with you."

"Oh yeah," he replied. "Just lie down and relax." As I lay there, I heard him telling another guy, "He got shot in his left ribs by an RPG, and it punched in his left lung before the shrapnel exited out his back. He's also shot in the back. We need to get him prepped for the OR."

"What?" I said, the drowsiness lifting from a new adrenaline rush as we landed at the hospital. "You need to get me going! Just patch me up really quick so I can get back out there!" But nobody was listening to me. They started taking my pants off to prep me for surgery.

"I was shot on my left rib. You don't need to take my pants off!" I yelled. "I need them so I can get back out there on the ground with my team!" As they told me to calm down, we began arguing, and I ended up punching the medic. I was just so angry that no one was listening to me. I needed to get back out there in that fight! Why didn't they understand that?

A Heavenly Visitor

Even when we got to the medical base, I was still combative. I didn't want any morphine; I didn't want to go to surgery. I wanted to fight! My team needed me out there!

A young woman in an army uniform came to my bedside. I couldn't see her face, but something about her gave me a feeling of tranquility. Somehow, even though I could not see her features, I could sense that she was beautiful. She came up beside me and took my hand. Then she started rubbing my hair.

When I was a kid, sometimes I would get so angry with everything I thought was going wrong that I'd get into neighborhood fights. I'd get so angry that I'd want to hurt myself, my mom, or anyone who was near, but Mom would hold me down. Then she would hold my hand and rub my hair, just like this young woman was doing now.

She'd tell me that she loved me and that everything was going to be okay.

"I've got you," she'd say. "We're going to get through this." Even when I'd fight her and tell her I hated her, she'd just calmly say, "I know," and would just continue to try to soothe me. She'd never leave me, even when I felt mad at her and blamed her for everything bad in my childhood.

The woman in the army uniform had the same calming presence. She kept saying, "I've got you. We're going to get through this." She smelled like beautiful wildflowers just after a fresh rain or the morning dew. The closer she leaned in to comfort me, the stronger the scent became, as if her hair were a spring meadow filled with wildflowers. The smell alone gave me such a sense of calm, as if I were being held in a warm embrace but could still feel the cooling touch of the dew.

> *I believe that angel was looking out for me. She told me I was going to be okay, and I believed it.*

I remember feeling such comfort that I didn't want to fight anymore. She told me to stop fighting, that it would be all right, and I drifted off, believing everything she was saying.

No Females on Base

A couple of days later, I woke up. A male nurse nearby saw me stir. "Oh, there's Muhammad Ali," he joked. "You worked a couple of people over pretty good! You even gave one of the doctors a black eye!"

"Oh, I'm sorry," I said.

"Nah, it's combat. Everyone understands."

"Hey, who was that female nurse that was here the day I came in?"

"Female nurse?" he asked.

"Yeah. She sat beside me and held my hand and rubbed my hair. She smelled like fresh wildflowers."

The nurse smirked, then laughed. "Nobody like that around here! Not that day."

"No, I swear! She held my hand."

"Dude, no one held your hand and no one rubbed your hair! We were laying ourselves across you, trying to hold you down because you threw the surgical tray to the ground and punched the doctor in the face! We weren't trying to hold your hand and rub your hair—we were trying to tie your hands down!"

"But there was a girl..."

"This is a combat hospital," he insisted. "There haven't been females here in the last couple of months."

"I know what I saw!" I said. But I couldn't convince him. I lay there in bed for a while, wondering if maybe he was right. I had never seen her face. But she had acted just like my mom had when I was a boy, like she knew exactly what she had to do to calm me down.

I don't know if my comforter was my guardian angel or some other type of angel, but it was definitely an angelic presence. I truly believe that. Some might say it was the effect of the drugs, but I believe that angel was looking out for me. When she told me that we were going to get through this, that I was going to be okay, I believed it. I wasn't scared. I didn't care what the doctors had to do. I was just thankful that she was there.

The Long Road Back

I wasn't well enough after surgery to go back to my unit, so I was sent to Germany for more recovery. I had developed an infection, which was worsened by the flight. The high altitude caused the infection to spread throughout my body more quickly. By the time we landed, I needed a blood transfusion. I was out for a couple more days.

When I woke up, I was told that I'd had more surgery and that soon I would need to begin physical therapy there in Germany. The doctors told me there was a good chance I'd be sent to Walter Reed Hospital in Washington and wind up being medically discharged. They said that because of my injury, I'd never really be able to wear body armor anymore, so I would be incapable of staying in the army.

I was given a rare opportunity to see a vision of a hoped-for future, but what did it mean?

What was a twenty-year-old man who was no good in school supposed to do if he couldn't be in the military? My whole life, I had never felt like I was really, naturally good at anything until I joined the army. Now I was going to be kicked out. How could the army not need me anymore? To say I was devastated or crushed would be an understatement.

The worry of losing my spot in the military overtook everything. I hardly gave a thought to what I'd seen when I was dying. I'd heard about people who said they had "crossed over" into heaven and had seen God, but I hadn't seen God, and I hadn't gone to heaven. I knew that I'd been given a rare opportunity to see alternative versions of my past and even a vision of a hoped-for future, but what did it all mean? What was I supposed to do with it? I put it all out of my mind. I couldn't try to process a supernatural vision. I was too caught up in the immediate concerns of the here and now.

For a while, all I could seem to do was wallow in self-pity and sadness. The physical pain itself was horrendous. I had to have my bandages changed frequently so the wounds would stay clean. I had almost a foot and a half of packing in my side that was replaced sometimes twice a day. It was excruciating. I think I could've stood it if I'd known I had a purpose to get back to when I recovered, but I felt that I'd lost my whole life. Without the army, I didn't know how to move forward.

I felt so bad that soon, the only thing I looked forward to was the morphine and the pills. I grew addicted to the feeling they gave me: they were the only way to numb myself to the world and to the physical pain. I refused to continue with my physical therapy. I didn't want to do anything except die. The doctors said they had no choice but to transfer me to Walter Reed to finish my therapy.

During this ordeal, my mom and Don never came to see me. I know now that they had been trying, but I didn't know it then. There was a lot of red tape to cut through with the Red Cross before they'd let them get to me in Germany, but no one relayed any of this information to me at the time, so my old, familiar anger took over. I decided to quit talking to them. *If they don't want to be here, then I don't want them to be here either!* I told myself. Deep down inside, I felt like a little kid who just wanted his mom and dad, but I felt like they'd abandoned me. Well, if they weren't going to try, I decided, then neither was I.

One night in Germany, shortly before I was due to be shipped out to Walter Reed, I decided I was done. I was in terrible physical pain, but also emotional turmoil. Now that I was no longer combat-fit, who was I? What purpose did I have on this earth? My only solace was in the morphine, the Vicodin, and the hydrocodone I was prescribed. But it wasn't enough. The meds numbed my body, but I wanted to numb myself to reality. I couldn't face the thought of having to go find something else to do once I was medically discharged.

The more drugs I got, the less concern I felt. The drugs freed me from the urge to do anything, even go outside. I didn't care about physical therapy; I didn't care about trying to stand back up or about talking or even eating. What reason did I have to try to do anything? Once I was out of the army, who would take care of me if I couldn't take care of myself and my parents didn't care anymore? All I wanted was to die, but I didn't have it in me to kill myself. I guess I hoped that the pills would somehow take me away so that I wouldn't have to deal with anything.

Rock Bottom

Each day when I woke up, I was disappointed to still be alive. I just wanted it all to be over. I had a morphine drip with a button I could push when I felt that I needed more pain relief, and I was pushing that button a lot. The doctors and nurses noticed.

"We're going to have to start limiting your morphine," they warned me. "You're taking more than you need, and you're not doing your physical therapy or talking to anyone." Eventually, they accused me of abusing the morphine and not adjusting.

"If you'll start back on your physical therapy and do the work, maybe we can put you back on a limited amount of morphine," they said. How could they do this to me? I couldn't walk! It took a full ten minutes for me to even be able to sit up in bed! They knew how replacing all that packing tortured me, and they didn't even care! "We can give you some Tylenol," they offered. *Wow, thanks a lot,* I thought.

The last straw was when the doctor tried changing my bandages when I wasn't on anything stronger than the Tylenol. His bedside manner was rough. He ripped the packing out of my side with no concern for the pain I was in. When I lost my temper with him, he reminded me that he outranked me and that I had to call him sir. But what really got to me was when he said, "You're supposed to be infantry? How about you act like it?"

I should have turned to God, but I was too distracted.

I can't think of anything worse anyone could've said to me at that point. All it did was remind me that I was completely disconnected now from my identity as a soldier. How dare he! Sure, he outranked me, but he'd never seen real combat. He wasn't the one lying in a hospital bed all shot up and useless. And what was the point of acting like I was in the infantry when the military was kicking me out?

The rest of that night, I seethed with anger. The medical staff gave me nothing but Tylenol every four hours. It wasn't the physical pain that was really killing me, though. It was the emotional pain. I felt that the drugs were the only way I had to cope. I should've turned to God, but I was too distracted, I guess. Oh, I prayed...just not for the right things. I'd pray that someone would find a way to get me more drugs.

I even tried to make a few "side deals" with God: I'll do this if you'll give me this. But God wasn't buying what I was selling.

I'd been in the hospital for two and a half weeks. Because my abdomen was so torn up from my injury, I couldn't walk well. And since I wasn't doing my physical therapy, my legs were getting weaker from disuse. But I wasn't paralyzed. I could get out of that bed...with the right motivation.

I was letting this beat me; I was mentally weak, lost in self-pity.

It took me quite a while to sit up and then get out of bed, but I managed to scoot over to a wheelchair. I sat in the wheelchair for some time to catch my breath again. I hooked my IV to a mobile unit. It took me nearly half an hour to wheel myself to the room next door, where another soldier lay in bed with a morphine drip.

The soldier in that bed wasn't really moving. He had a bad leg injury from an IED and was pretty much out cold from the pain medicine.

I'm just going to take as much as I need, and then I'll give it back to him, I told myself. I tried not to face the fact that I was taking pain medicine away from a guy who really needed it just because I'd chosen to give up. But I couldn't ignore the truth: I was motivated enough to get myself up just so I could steal someone else's drugs.

Guilt washed over me. It was pretty sad to realize that the only time I had pushed myself was to do something this low. I was willing to steal the thing that controlled this soldier's physical pain just so I could use it to block out my mental pain. I was letting this beat me; I was mentally weak, lost in self-pity. I knew I needed to do better. But before

I could decide to do the right thing, I was caught. The medical staff yelled at me and looked at me like I was less than human. I'd hit rock bottom, and I'd never felt so ashamed.

When I had time to reflect on how far I'd fallen, the thing that really scared me about it all was the thought that I was turning into Lloyd. I was using drugs as a crutch. I couldn't believe what I'd done. I was letting a substance control me! I'd wanted to fight for the drugs more than I wanted to fight to get up out of bed.

I lay in the hospital bed the rest of the night, thinking about Lloyd's addiction. He did so many different drugs. I started wondering, *What if this is how it started with Lloyd? What if it was something seemingly small and simple, a little moral compromise that snowballed into bigger compromises, until the next thing he knew, he became a neglectful, abusive father?* This should've been a catalyst for change, but instead, I started thinking that it was my inescapable destiny to become just like Lloyd. I felt like I had no way to crawl out from underneath the weight of my own addiction. I didn't want to take the drugs, but I craved them so badly. When they were taken away, I was willing to do almost anything to get them back.

If I was going to end up like Lloyd eventually, I decided there was no point in even trying to fight it now. The family I'd seen in that vision... there was no point in living for that if I'd only destroy it. There was no point in even trying. The thought made me angry, but it also made me want the drugs even more to make the thought go away. When I'd seen that vision of a loving family of my own in that pool, I had wanted to fight so hard for that. But now I felt that having such love and admiration from a wife and children was an unreachable dream.

Hope Returns

After I'd been caught trying to steal the medicine, the hospital sent a liaison to talk with me. I wish I could remember her name. She was completely different in her manner than the doctor who'd reminded me I was no longer in the infantry.

"Let's go outside," she suggested. I didn't see much point but decided I'd humor her.

Having someone to talk to helped me feel better in spite of myself.

For the first time since I'd arrived in Germany, I was able to see how beautiful the country truly was. Just as I'd tried to block out reality, I'd also blocked out the world around me: the entire time, I'd had the windows closed and the blinds shut in my hospital room. Every day had felt like an eternity.

The liaison pushed me in my wheelchair all around the complex for about an hour. "You know," she said, "I could help you do stuff."

"You can't do anything for a guy in a wheelchair," I said.

"You're not crippled," she replied. "You just have to get up and move."

I liked that she talked to me like I was a human being—like I was a person and not just a burden. She came every day and pushed my wheelchair around outside for a full hour.

Somewhere along the way, I felt a small flicker of motivation, like maybe I could do something again. But whenever that feeling started to rise up inside me, I reminded myself that it was just her job to make me feel this way. It was her job to take me outside; she didn't really believe in me personally. Soldiers were coming in all the time from Afghanistan and Iraq. The hospital was getting full, and the doctors just wanted to get me out. I wouldn't allow myself to think the liaison actually cared about me as a person. Still, having someone to talk to helped me feel better in spite of myself.

Back at the hospital, the medical staff told me I had two options: I could go to Walter Reed and do my therapy, or I might be allowed to go back to my duty station in Hawaii and complete physical therapy there. Either way, when therapy was over, I'd most likely be medically discharged. One day, I told the liaison during our walk that it wasn't a real choice; either way, I was out of the army.

"Look," she said. "I've seen a lot of people in your situation. If you go to Walter Reed, it's almost one hundred percent guaranteed that you're going to be medically discharged. It's a great facility that provides great medical treatment for soldiers, but it's the end of the road for your military career. If you're allowed to go back to your duty station, that means that the army still feels that they have an opportunity to get you back into service. It's solely up to you."

"I want to go back to Hawaii!" I said. "I want to have a chance!"

"You have to be able to sit up on your own, hold yourself up, and sit without back support for two minutes," she explained. "Then you have to be able to stand up and walk unassisted. Are you willing to try to get there?"

I wanted to try. But over the next few days and weeks, the task seemed impossible. Whenever I tried to sit up, my abs and back would spasm, and the pain was blinding. It was useless. I was bound for Walter Reed. I couldn't do it.

Little did I know that the day I decided to give up, my brother, who'd just graduated from high school, was having a going-away party before he left for the marines. It had been four weeks since my injury. Mom called so I could speak to John before he shipped out. I was still mad at Mom for not coming to see me in Germany, so usually when she called, I ignored it, but for some reason that day, I answered. I'm not sure if I just wanted someone to pick a fight with or if I was just so lonely that I was willing to swallow my pride, but I picked up the phone.

Mom chatted for a while and told me all about the party. Then she told me that their friend, Tony, had come to the party and had brought his daughter, a college student in Muncie.

"She's so easy to talk to," Mom said. "I think you'd really like her. It'd be nice for you to make a new friend your own age. She said she'd love to talk to you and that you could call her sometime if you wanted."

"Don't try to fix me up with anybody, Mom!" I complained.

"It's not like that," she insisted. "She's just someone different to talk to."

"Fine. Give me her name and number."

Her name was Jen Hershaw. And for the next week, I left her number sitting there untouched while I wallowed in self-pity. I was still reeling from the pain in my body and from the shame of having tried just a few days earlier to steal the other soldier's morphine.

Then one day, when it was particularly dark outside, I was tired of being alone. I could buzz a nurse if I needed something, but they couldn't just stay and talk. It was evening, and the liaison was already gone. Everyone else had a life and was able to move around. Meanwhile,

I was stuck in a hospital room with nothing to do and no one to talk to. I could feel myself emotionally reaching for...something...but I didn't know what. I decided to call Jen and see what happened.

I could feel myself emotionally reaching for...something...but I didn't know what.

A lovely voice said hello.

"Is this Jen?" I asked.

"Yes," she replied. "Who's this?"

"Oh, I'm sorry. This is Bud Evans. I thought my parents had told you I was going to call you. But I don't want you to feel like you have to talk to me."

"Oh, not at all! But I'm at work, so I can't really talk right now," she said. "Can I call you back in about an hour when I get off?"

"Sure," I said. But in my head, I was thinking, *Yeah, right. Whatever. She's never going to call me back.*

But a little over an hour later, she did call back.

Conversation flowed so easily between us. We couldn't believe our parents had been friends all these years, and yet we'd never met. The only reason she even knew what I looked like was because she'd seen my senior portrait at the house during John's going-away party. After we got off the phone, I had a better night than I'd had in weeks.

A couple of days later, I called Jen back. We talked for three hours! One of the things I learned about her was that she had a deep, abiding faith in God. It was the most important thing in her life. I told her how I'd started out viewing God as my enemy at first, then how I had begrudgingly come to love Him and had given my life to Him. But I admitted that my faith had grown cold, especially after the distraction of the military and combat, not to mention this injury. She said she'd pray that God would strengthen my faith. I thought that was nice of her to say, but I didn't really think too much about it.

It felt amazing to know that I could feel comfortable trusting Jen.

I shared things with Jen I'd never told anybody before. I told her all about my childhood. I even told her about being shot and finding myself in the pool with the visions. I'd told Mom, Don, and John some of it, and they'd believed it was a gift from God, but I hadn't told them all the details. I told Jen more of the complete story (leaving out the last and most important vision of the wife so as not to scare her off), and I also told her about the female nurse who'd calmed me down by rubbing my hair. I explained how the male nurses all told me there were no females on base and that I must've been seeing things because of the morphine but that I wondered if she'd been an angel.

"You probably think I'm crazy or something," I said.

"No," she said. "I believe you. That's incredible."

It felt amazing to know that I could feel comfortable trusting Jen like that, so I even shared with her my fears. I told her how terrified I was about being discharged, how scared I was at the thought of trying to go to college because I'd never done well in school. I told her about my option to go to Walter Reed or back to my duty station in Hawaii.

"Why not try for Hawaii?" Jen asked. "If I had a choice between Washington or Hawaii, I know which one I'd pick!"

"Yeah, but it's not that easy," I told her.

"Come on, Bud," Jen said. "You fought your whole childhood, you fought in Iraq, and now you've fought through all this! Getting to Hawaii should be easy for you."

To be honest, that made me a little defensive. It was easy for her to say; she didn't know how excruciating it was just to try to sit up! I tried to explain why I couldn't do it.

"Wouldn't you rather try versus not try?" Jen asked.

"It's better to just accept it," I argued.

"Bud, you never sounded like a quitter before, and now you're quitting?"

That hit me hard. That night, after I got off the phone with Jen, I started doing physical therapy in my bed. Each day after that, I pushed myself harder and harder. The more Jen and I talked, the better I started feeling. I got excited about my recovery and even more excited about my phone calls with Jen, which became a regular nightly thing. Soon, I was able to complete the tasks needed to get me to Hawaii. I couldn't believe it!

I didn't really think about whether or not I felt attracted to Jen. She was just someone I could talk to without judgment. Hearing her believe in me was different than when my parents assured me I was going to make it. They were supposed to say those things, but she didn't have to. If Jen felt like I should be fighting, then I felt like I should too.

The Comeback

Four months had passed since I'd been shot in Iraq. Now I was on my way back to Hawaii. My deployment in Iraq was supposed to have been for a full year, but I'd completed only six months of it before my injury. After I finished the physical therapy program back at my duty station, I asked to be sent back to Iraq for six months. Part of my reason for asking was that I wanted to finish what I'd started; the other part was that I needed confirmation that I wasn't combat-disabled.

Meanwhile, I stayed in contact with Jen. We weren't falling completely in love yet, but the attraction was building. I knew I had feelings for her, but I also knew I loved the military. From time to time, I'd think back to the family I'd seen in the pool when I was dying on the field in Iraq. I started wondering if Jen could be the wife I'd seen in my vision, if she could be the mother of the children whose voices I'd heard. I didn't know for sure, but I knew that Jen was definitely someone special. I suppose if I'd been in better contact with God, He might have revealed to me what He was doing for me through Jen, but I just wasn't in the right spiritual place at that time to recognize how He was working in my life.

> *I just wasn't in the right spiritual place at that time to recognize how He was working in my life.*

Even though I cared for Jen, I refused to let my feelings for her keep me from returning to Iraq. In fact, she was the whole reason I was able to return at all. She was the one who'd motivated me to get moving again and to try when I wasn't sure I could do it. I decided not to tell her I was going back because I was afraid she'd try to stop me. I called one day and was relieved to get her voice mail so that she couldn't ask me any questions.

I left a message, saying, "Hey, I got a little bit of training I'm supposed to be doing. I should be able to call you back in a couple of days." It was going to be more like two weeks, but I felt like I had to follow through with my plan.

Going back to Iraq for the second time was invigorating. I had a whole new drive for the military. I completely forgot how angry I'd been that they'd wanted to kick me out. If I'd thought being a soldier felt great the first time around, it was nothing compared to this feeling of getting "back on the horse." The second time felt better than the first time because I was returning a hero.

Going back to finish serving after being shot garnered a lot of respect from fellow soldiers. High-ranking and noncommissioned officers commended me and expressed their gratitude for my service. It felt amazing. I wouldn't go so far as to say I felt untouchable, but I felt that my path was now paved for a successful career in the military.

It didn't take long, though, before it became clear to me that I wasn't really back to my old self 100 percent. When I put on body armor again, it just didn't feel right. It compressed around my ribs, and I could feel it squeezing my lungs. It was so irritating to my scar tissue that I wound up developing an abscess. It would have to be removed to keep the infection from spreading. The thing was, the military didn't put soldiers under for medical procedures unless it was a life-or-death situation. Mine was not.

That night, I went to the med tent, and the doctor injected me with a numbing agent to help with the pain a little bit. Then he started cutting me open. It hurt, but not as much as having my bandages and packing changed after my initial injury. But I was fully aware that the doctor was cutting me open, so that was unnerving to say the least.

All of a sudden, we started getting mortar fire, right in the middle of my surgery! We had to evacuate the tent. The medical team grabbed a plastic tarp, and I had to walk out, holding a piece of plastic over my incision with one hand, and holding some of my equipment and my rifle with the other. We went inside a bunker, and the nurse laid out the tarp on the dirt floor. The doctor turned on a headlamp and finished the surgery. Then he sewed me up as the bombing continued.

I felt a small flicker of my spirit come to life again.

All I knew at that moment was that I had to talk to Jen. We were allowed only ten minutes on the phone, and the timing was pretty terrible, but I made the call. When Jen answered, I said, "I don't have a lot of time, but I can't wait. I want to talk to you." A mortar shell dropped at that very moment, and Jen could hear it.

"Was that a bomb?" she asked.

"I've got to go," I said.

I guess I can be pretty hardheaded because getting my attention required literally dropping a bomb, but something started to click for me that night. I can't really explain what it was, but after months of focusing only on getting drugs and then getting well and then getting back into the army, something shifted inside me. I felt a small flicker of my spirit come to life again. Almost imperceptible, but still there.

The next night, I was on tower guard with another soldier who, let's just say, wasn't the most religious of guys. We started talking about our lives, and I told him about Jen. What he said shocked me.

"Do you think you met her because...I mean..." He struggled to find the words. "It just sounds like you're pretty lucky or something. Kinda looks like God is looking out for you."

I could hardly believe what I was hearing. I'd never heard this fellow talk about God before, ever, yet here he was, explaining to me, the supposed Christian, how God was working in my life!

I'd spent most of my life trying to understand God's timing. I knew He could do anything whenever He wanted to, so it had always made me angry that He didn't do things for me when I wanted them. I'd felt that He hadn't gotten me away from Lloyd soon enough or that He hadn't helped me find my way soon enough or that He'd taken away the one thing I'd been good at way too soon. I hadn't pondered my old questions about God's timing versus my timing for quite a while, but now those thoughts came back to me. I knew in my heart that God knew more than I ever could and that His understanding far surpassed mine.

What the other guard said about God looking out for me made me see that I'd been so selfish all this time, thinking that I'd been the one to get myself to my duty station to finish my physical therapy, that I'd been the one to fight my way back into the military after my injury. That I'd been the one to swim up out of that pool to have another chance at life. But it was the grace of God that had provided me with these opportunities, these moments. It wasn't me. I might have done my part, but it was God who had given me the opportunities when He saw it was the right time. And yet, I hadn't seen it. I'd kept God on the back burner while I went about my own business.

All this time, I'd thought getting to know Jen was just happenstance.

"You're right," I told my fellow guard.

I thought about what might have happened to me if God had not put Jen in my life, if she had not pushed me to get up out of that hospital bed and try to make something of myself again. I could have been discharged and fallen completely into drug addiction and wound up on the streets, still feeling sorry for myself. But like this guy said, God was looking out for me.

God was looking out for me.

A New Path

My last couple of months in Iraq, the fighting was as intense as ever. My old self would have lived for the adrenaline rush of it all. I would have been completely in my element. But as much as I still loved the military, I now knew what was missing in my life.

During a mission, a fellow soldier said, "Evans, your tour's about up. You gonna reenlist?"

I knew if I stayed in the military, I could be successful. In some ways, I felt like I was born to be a soldier. I was good at it. And going back to Iraq after suffering such a huge injury had definitely secured my future in the army. No way the army could say I wasn't combat-fit after six months of successful missions post-injury. But I thought of that vision in the pool—the family who'd told me they loved me.

"I'm going to get out," I found myself saying.

Later, when I had the chance to make a phone call, I called my mom. "I'm going to marry Jen," I told her.

"Are you sure?" Mom asked. "You two still haven't met in person yet!" It wasn't that Mom didn't like Jen. They'd actually become good friends, not only because Jen's dad had been my parents' friend for years, but also because I made most of my ten-minute calls to Jen. She'd call Mom afterward and catch her up on how I was doing.

"Oh, I'm sure," I replied. I arranged to send Mom money to buy an engagement ring. She suggested putting a diamond from my great-grandmother's wedding band in the setting to make it extra special. This would all be news to Jen. I hadn't even told her I loved her!

When my tour was over and I was shipped back to Hawaii, I remember calling Jen one night. There was a five-hour time difference between us, and I remember being pretty tired. I guess that's why I let my guard down. At the end of the call, I said, "Okay, I'll talk to you later. I love you. Bye." When I realized what I'd said, I hung up in a panic. I hadn't wanted to tell her that over the phone. We'd never even met face-to-face! What if she thought I was crazy?

Immediately Jen called me back. "Did you say something at the end of our talk?" she asked.

"No, no," I replied. "I think I just said I'd talk to you tomorrow. Goodbye."

"Okay," Jen said. Just before she hung up, she added, "And by the way, I love you too."

When she said the words, "I love you," they sounded eerily familiar. It was the voice I'd heard in my vision of my future! Jen's voice! And the feeling her words gave me was the same feeling that had engulfed me that day in the cylindrical pool. I could feel the warmth of her love and the reassurance that she would always be there.

I called her right back.

"I've been wanting to tell you for months," she confessed.

"Well, why didn't you say anything?" I asked.

"What took you so long?"

Everything locked into place for me in that moment; I knew what my life was meant to be.

We both laughed and then talked for another three hours. No ten-minute phone call limits outside combat zones, thankfully! I had leave coming up, so I planned a trip home so that Jen and I could meet in person. We arranged for her to pick me up at the airport.

A Face-to-Face Meeting

When I got off the plane, I saw Jen before she saw me. She had long, straight, dark hair. She was wearing a white T-shirt with jean capris and flip-flops. Nothing fancy, yet she was so beautiful. When we made eye contact, the moment took my breath away. Everything locked into place for me in that moment; I knew what my life was meant to be. She would be my wife, and our family would be number one. They'd never have to compete for me with the military, as much as I loved it. Finally coming face-to-face with Jen made everything crystal clear. *Thank You, God,* I thought. *Thank You for everything that is happening.*

I felt a mixture of both fear and excitement that day. Jen and I were supposed to meet my whole extended family at five o'clock that evening for dinner, but we were so wrapped up in conversation on the drive that we missed our exit twice, and on that stretch of interstate, we had to go miles out of our way to get back, both times. We wound up being several hours late.

"Your family is going to hate me!" Jen said. She hadn't met most of my family yet, and she was afraid they'd blame her for not getting me to dinner on time.

"No, they won't," I said. "And if they do, I don't care. This is the best car ride I've ever had."

For the rest of my leave, whenever we weren't with my family, Jen and I were together. A couple of days after that first in-person meeting, I took her to the river, where I got down on one knee and proposed. She said yes.

I'd already decided to leave the military. I didn't think I could be the husband and father I wanted to be while still being active duty. I had to be all-in for the army or all-in for a family of my own.

Although I didn't ponder my vision much, the memory of the future family I could have was always in my mind. I felt like God hadn't shown me that vision for nothing, and it helped me make the decision not to continue in the army. I won't lie, though. It was hard to walk away. The army had offered me a $20,000 tax-free bonus, a promotion to staff sergeant, and a position as team leader to reenlist in Iraq. But a family of my own, the family I'd seen in my vision, would be priceless.

Family Man

I got out of the army in January 2006, when I was twenty-two, and Jen and I were married the next month. Our first order of business— well, Jen's first order of business, to be honest—was finding a church and getting involved. I admit I was spiritually lazy at the time and didn't see the rush to join a congregation, but I didn't want Jen to go by herself. Thanks to her good influence, we went regularly and spent more time reading the Bible, and I could feel myself growing in the Lord.

The memory of that intense feeling of love washed over me.

Jen continued her college coursework and became a teacher. I found a job working with troubled teenagers for a few years, and later I sold tires. In 2018, I decided to go to back to school. It was scary, given my history with school, but I wanted to become a physical therapy assistant. Physical therapy was what had gotten me back to being combat-fit, and I wanted to help wounded soldiers at a Veterans' Administration hospital get their lives back too.

One day, just shy of three years into our marriage, Jen woke me early one morning.

"Look at this!" she said. She was holding a piece of white plastic about the size of a Popsicle stick.

"What is it?" I asked. To be honest, I was a little annoyed to be woken up for a guessing game. I was so groggy that it took a few moments before I understood what the stick meant. "We're going to have a baby?" I yelled. I was so excited that I jumped out of bed and started naming off everyone I wanted to call.

"We can't tell anyone yet!" Jen said. "It's too early."

"Too early? No way! You can't tell me we're going to have a baby and then expect me not to tell the whole world!"

A few months later, we learned we were having a baby girl. I didn't care if we had a girl or a boy; I just knew I wanted two children. But when we learned it was a girl, I was so excited and couldn't do enough for Jen and to get everything prepped and ready for my little princess.

But in the back of my mind, I thought of Lloyd. The thought still tormented me that somehow it might be my destiny to wind up just like him. I was terrified that I would be the kind of father he had been. Jen assured me that would never happen, that I was nothing like Lloyd. I wanted to believe her, but when I finally held baby Callie in my arms, I couldn't help but be afraid. I wanted more than anything to be the father she deserved, but what if I failed?

When Callie grabbed my finger for the first time with her tiny little hand, it was like I was back in that pool again. The memory of that intense feeling of love washed over me. I felt so much peace. The only difference was that this time, there was no fear of not having the vision come true. I was living it.

When I would hold my baby daughter, I would often think about growing up in Las Vegas and what my life had been like then. Now, here I was, so far away from all that. When I was being beaten as a child, I could never have envisioned myself as a grown man, getting up in the middle of the night to change my baby girl's diaper and holding her and soothing her back to sleep. But God saw it all, long before I could even fathom it. God knew all along.

When we found out a couple of years later that Jen was pregnant again—this time with a boy—I could hardly believe it. Two kids. A girl and a boy. Just like in my vision. Not that I would've complained over two girls or two boys—I was so grateful just to have healthy children. But the fact that I'd seen this before...it was incredible.

God hadn't shown me that vision to torment me about what I would never have; He was trying to show me a reason not to quit and to keep fighting. So much had happened since that experience that had taken up so much of my attention that I suppose I hadn't really given it the attention it deserved. But the vision remained clear in my memory, and now, finally, the impact was undeniable. I could still see the scenes I saw in the pool, still smell the flowers and feel the warm embrace of the angel who'd stayed by my bedside in the military hospital.

A Lingering Impact

As I grew in my faith, I wanted to share with others how great God had been to me personally. I started telling people about what God had done for me that day on the battlefield, how He'd given me the vision of my future. Of course I'd already shared the story with Mom and Don and John, but I started telling members of our extended family. Most of them would listen, but I wasn't always sure they believed me. I also started telling friends, even those who didn't believe in God. To my surprise, some of even the most nonreligious would say, "I believe that could've happened."

Even though I couldn't see the faces of my family in the vision, I'm convinced it was Jen and our children. Even now, after about fifteen years of marriage, whenever Jen and I go somewhere, just the two of us, it still feels to me like it's our first date. I want to get the door for her and remind her how special she is. I want to put her above anyone else.

I will never forget the feeling of hopelessness I felt inside that pool when I thought that vision of my family would never come to pass. It was absolutely horrifying to think of losing it. Now that God has granted this life to me, I never want to take any of it for granted. I loved the military, and I'm thankful for my time in the service. I definitely still miss it, but it doesn't come close to this life I'm living now with Jen and our two children. I love where I am, and I want to keep God first and keep our family strong in faith.

I love where I am, and I want to keep God first and keep our family strong in faith.

A couple of years ago, I felt that I was getting further away from God than I should be, so I was baptized again. Not only did I feel the need in my heart to rededicate my life to Christ, I also wanted to set an example for my kids. I wanted that feeling of having my sins washed away, of being clean again. Our daughter made the decision to follow Jesus and be baptized just a few months after I was re-baptized, and our son is growing in his understanding and clarity of the gospel, so I expect that he will soon make the same decision as well. I've tried to teach them both that every second given to us is given by God—it's not something that we earned ourselves.

I think that's been the biggest blessing of almost dying: the gratitude. When I see parents who mistreat their kids or don't treasure their relationships, it just doesn't make sense to me. How can they not realize that their families are such a gift from God? If we all realized that, families would always treat one another in the best way possible. We'd watch what we say and do and guard our families with everything we have.

It breaks my heart to see people so carelessly destroy such a blessing. Through my experience, God helped me to see the importance of truly valuing the people I love and each moment I have with them.

Having said all this, I am still so afraid of turning into Lloyd one day. Whenever I make a mistake, my first thought is, *What if Jen leaves me*? I'm always so afraid I'll lose the gift of my family. I beat myself up whenever I fall short—even if it's just making a B instead of an A on a test. The only reason Jen and I ever argue, honestly, is when she has to convince me that she won't leave me and take the kids and go find someone more deserving of them.

> *It was God who gave me the ability to move, the ability to continue.*

Another important lesson I learned the day that I lay bleeding on the ground in Iraq was that when we overcome something, it's not by our own strength. I'd always seen myself as tough for surviving my childhood with Lloyd. But it dawned on me one day that this view of things was, in essence, giving Lloyd the credit for my success. When I was a young man in the army and I got through trials such as the road march—carrying such weight and moving my legs forward when I didn't think it was humanly possible to keep going—I used to feel proud of myself. But it wasn't me, and it certainly wasn't Lloyd or his influence that got me through basic training or anything else. It was God who gave me the ability to move; it was God who gave me the ability to continue.

When I was twenty-seven, I heard that Lloyd was in bad health and probably wouldn't be around much longer. I decided it might be my last chance to reach out to him for closure. I wanted to know why he'd done the things he did to us.

When I called and identified myself, I could immediately hear in his voice that time had not mellowed him. Even though his body had been destroyed by years of drug abuse, he was severely overweight, and he was requiring home health care, he couldn't accept that he was dying.

I guess I shouldn't have been surprised that I couldn't get the answers I sought; after all, it wasn't like Lloyd to be concerned about anyone else. He tried to turn the conversation to how John and I had hurt him by changing our last name. He said he'd had no choice but to beat us because we'd been such bad kids. Then he started blaming my mom for everything, claiming that his behavior was all her fault—like she made him beat us, somehow controlling him even when she was away at work. He refused to take any responsibility for his own actions. In his mind, he was the victim.

Even though I didn't get the resolution I wanted, I'm glad I talked to Lloyd before he died. It allowed me to see him from an adult's point of view and to know once and for all that his actions were not my fault or anyone else's. He chose his own path, and I have to choose mine. The one I choose will always go in the opposite direction from his.

From the day I gave my life to Jesus as a young teenager, my faith has not always been steadfast. But as I grow and mature in years, I feel that I'm growing and maturing as a Christian as well. What I saw that day in Iraq was so far beyond me. Given my injury, I shouldn't even be alive today. But I did not save myself and I didn't just get lucky. God saved me. And not only did He save my life, but He also gave me that moment to see my future. I know it wasn't some kind of fluke. I believe I was meant to get shot that day and see what I saw. I'd spent all those years in anger, asking, "Why me?" And it was as if God told me, "I'm going to answer that for you."

Sometimes we don't like what God shows us. When I saw my childhood again, it made me furious. I thought I'd already worked for years to deal with all that, and then there it was, right in my face, forcing me to relive every negative emotion all over again. It was all so strong and so real. It was like seeing a grisly car accident but not being able to look away. But God also showed me glimpses of my family in Indiana and gave me all those good feelings again too. He showed me the moment in my past where I decided I was done letting other people control my life.

God saved my life so that I could develop a closer relationship with Him.

Through all this, God showed me that my life was so much more than just the struggles in Las Vegas. My life also had successes and good things to come. When He showed me the option for my future with my wife and children, I didn't need to see anything else. Of all the visions, it was the clearest, and the one that gave me the hope to push myself to start swimming up, back into my body so that I could live for the future God had prepared for me.

If I had died on that battlefield in Iraq, I would have missed out on the life I'd always wanted here on earth. But even more important, I wouldn't be ready for what will come after this life. I was young and self-centered then, and I wasn't putting God first. I was caught up in the here and now, the temporary things instead of the eternal things that truly matter. But God saved my life so that I could develop a closer relationship with Him. He gave me a godly wife who pushed me to grow spiritually and helped me come closer to becoming the man He wants me to be.

Of course I'm not perfect, and I pray that I will continue to mature as a Christian every day that I'm allowed to continue living, but I do know that I never take for granted the blessings God has bestowed on me. Jesus Christ, my Savior, pulled me out of the anger and shame that held me down, and He gave me a new life and a new hope.

The next time I leave my earthly body, I will know exactly where I am headed. And by the grace of God, I will be ready.

My Life since My
Near-Death Experience

Bud Evans

It's been over fifteen years since my NDE. It occurred in 2005, just eleven or so hours before my twentieth birthday.

Q *How long after the NDE did you talk about it? Who did you share it with? What kind of reaction did you get and how did that make you feel?*

A I started opening up about my NDE with my parents early in 2006, but I didn't tell them the entire story. They were overwhelmed and tearful. My brother says my experience has strengthened his faith. He says my story motivates him and that he wishes he could be more like me.

When my now-wife, Jen, and I first started talking, I didn't want to freak her out by telling her she might have been the wife I saw in my NDE. I told her parts of it, but it was a couple of years into our relationship before I told her all of it.

I've told friends who are atheists, and they don't believe the vision came from God; they think my brain was coping with the trauma. I think their reaction is just a lack of faith.

Q *What has been the biggest challenge in returning to an earthly life after your NDE?*

A I struggle with feeling that I am not good enough for my family. I am terrified of turning out like my biological father, Lloyd. My wife and other family members will say, "Oh, you'll never be like Lloyd," but I'm sure Lloyd didn't want to be the way he was either. Lloyd did a number on my self-esteem, and I never want to do that to my kids. God showed me in my NDE that I could be a good father and have all the wonderful things in my life that I have, but it's still hard to accept that as true. I work hard every day to be the kind of husband and father I ought to be.

Q Has the intensity of your NDE lessened since you've been back in your earthly life?

A My NDE was a very pivotal moment in my life, and it shaped the person I am today. I wonder sometimes if I had lived but had not seen that moment if I would be on a different path.

I don't think the intensity of the NDE will ever diminish. I will always value it and can't wait to tell my grandchildren about it. One of my biggest fears is that I'm going to die and it will be forgotten. Having my story in this book is a gift that God gave to me, and I'm thankful for it.

Q In reliving your NDE, do you recall aspects of it that at the time didn't make sense but now do? What were those?

A Most of the vision in the pool made sense, but the nurse in the hospital who held my hand was probably the hardest to understand because everyone told me she hadn't been there. Everything about her was real—the way she smelled like wildflowers and the way she picked up my hand and ran her fingers through my hair to calm me down. The medical staff said there was no one there doing that, but I could feel her hands and her fingernails lightly brushing over my scalp, relaxing me. I felt so much peace. It blows my mind that they insisted she was never there, but I'm confident she was. I couldn't see her face, but that didn't bother me at all. I have faith that she was an angel sent to me.

Q *Is there a person you wish you had seen in your NDE?*

A I would have liked to see my Grandpa Walter, my mom's stepdad. He was alive during my NDE, but he and my grandma moved to Minnesota after we moved to Indiana, so I didn't see them much.

I never shared this story with Grandpa Walter. I wish he could have somehow been in the vision to talk to me, though, so that I could have asked him for advice during that NDE moment. He was a real stabilizing influence on John and me as kids. I never felt afraid when Grandpa Walter was around.

Q *How did your NDE change your relationship with God, your family, and friends?*

A It took a while for the NDE to bring about a surge in my faith. I was thankful for it, but I was twenty years old and in the infantry, living fast and hard.

Before the NDE and after my recovery, I worked out hard and I drank hard. Every now and then I would think of the NDE and think I should slow down, but I felt even more bulletproof after the injury because I hadn't died. During active duty in the military, it was easy to get distracted and be pulled away by the devil.

When I fell for Jen, I knew she was the one I was supposed to be with, and I knew that if I wanted to have the family I'd seen in my vision, I had to give up military life. The NDE made me realize where I wanted to be. If I had stayed in active duty, I probably would have continued to be distracted by the here and now and wouldn't have really let the NDE impact me the way it has. That means I probably wouldn't have the walk with God that I have now, partly because Jen helps me to stay focused and close to the Lord.

Q *You were upset with your mom and Don while you were in the hospital in Germany. Were you able to resolve your feelings with them when you got home?*

A When I was in the hospital, I was really mad at myself and everything that was going on, and I felt like it was everyone else's fault. I didn't want to talk to Mom and Don, but Jen helped me change my attitude. When I started to feel better, I could see things more clearly and realized none of it was Mom and Don's fault.

Don, who I call Dad, has been the only father to me. My relationship with him and my mom is great now, and I cherish my parents and their love. We have our problems, but we work them out like adults and move on.

I used to be very angry at the past, and I still struggle with adjusting to what happened, but I know that I have my parents, my wife, and my kids beside me to help me.

Every Moment Matters

By Andrew Garcia, as told to Stephanie Thompson

Remembering the goodness of God in the past will help us in seasons where it's harder to see Him.

Esther Fleece

Today's the day," I whispered and smiled at my sleepy six-year-old daughter, Cara. A huge grin erupted across her face.

"It's my birthday party day, Daddy!" she said, tossing back her bedsheets. She stood on the mattress and threw her arms around my neck. I hugged her tightly and breathed in the sweet scent of her long, dark hair. Grabbing her waist, I lifted her high above my head, almost to the ceiling. She giggled as her little legs flutter kicked beneath her unicorn sleep dress.

Now a kindergartner, Cara was about to have her first big birthday bash—very different from the kinds of birthday parties I had as a child. Of course, it was a different time—the 1980s—and my parents struggled financially. Most of the birthday parties I had as a child were low key and modest, usually with family members.

My wife, Natalie, and I had financial struggles, too, but we tried to pour positive experiences into Cara and our three-year-old son, Corban. We wanted to make sure they felt secure, valued, and loved. Even though I knew my parents loved me, I was pretty insecure as a child. A short, chubby kid, I was teased a lot.

I knew how it felt to be an underdog. Maybe that's how I developed a heart for people.

I grew up in a semitraditional Mexican American family. I say semitraditional because even though we lived in the Hispanic area of town and most of my friends were Hispanic, we didn't speak Spanish in our home. My full-blooded Mexican parents had been exposed to bias and prejudice all their lives. That colored the way they raised my two older brothers and me.

We lived in the small town of Gilroy, California, garlic capital of the world, just outside San Jose. Our neighborhood was on the wrong side of the tracks, literally, because the freight train route that ran through town divided it into two sections. My family lived on the poor side of the tracks, in an area that was run-down, with lots of violence, illegal drugs, and gang activity.

My parents met as migrant workers in Gilroy. My father's family was from Texas, and my mother's came from the Los Angeles area. They, with their families, followed the crop harvests and ended up in Gilroy each summer. Like most immigrants, their parents came to America hoping for a better life, with better economic and educational opportunities. Attaining that meant a lot of hard work.

Mom managed a coffee shop and worked retail jobs. Dad worked for General Electric, enrolled in college, and earned a master's degree in

Christian counseling. He became an associate minister for a predominantly white congregation when I was about five. Thanks to hard work and his education, Dad broke the mold of what was expected from someone who came from humble beginnings and of what had been the norm in his family.

Even so, my parents knew the struggles minorities faced. That's why they decided not to speak Spanish in our home. They wanted us to blend in as much as possible.

My family went to church on Sunday mornings, Sunday evenings, and Wednesday nights, but I wasn't close to God. I knew about God, but I didn't have an intimate, personal relationship with Him. I learned how to live in two worlds—with mostly white, Christian do-gooders and with disenfranchised minorities. I knew how it felt to be an underdog. Maybe that's how I developed a heart for people.

Questioning My Path

Natalie's father is a minister too. He and I serve together at First Baptist Church in Thousand Oaks, approximately forty miles from downtown Los Angeles. Natalie and I longed to create an environment where our kids would grow up feeling safe and included. For us, that meant being a part of a church and school community, and we found this with the small, tight-knit group of classmates and church friends in Thousand Oaks. Heck, our lives were so tight-knit that it was just a few paces between our home, our church, and the kids' school. We lived literally across the street.

After kissing my family goodbye that Saturday morning of Cara's birthday, I walked across the street to our church. The brisk fall air smelled fresh, thanks to an overnight rain shower. Even though it was late October, I wore shorts and a T-shirt—one of the perks of life in Southern California.

Cara's birthday party would be on the church's back patio in about an hour. Our church strived to be a beacon for the community and often opened its door for neighborhood events. My family was proud to be a part of it. Natalie and I both worked there. Cara attended kindergarten at the school too. Most weeks, we were on the church campus every day including Saturdays. And today we were having a Saturday birthday celebration there.

I'd already been over earlier to meet the delivery people with the rented bounce house. I showed them where to stake the giant castle on the lawn near the church's side patio. Cara would be so excited. She and her guests would have a blast.

That's when I noticed that the overnight rainstorm had blown twigs, leaves, and other debris onto the patio. I went to the work shed and pulled out the commercial leaf blower to clean things up before the guests arrived. After that, I wouldn't have much else to do. My in-laws were bringing balloons with them when they came a few minutes before the party. Natalie and I would carry over a piñata and the refreshments moments before the festivities began.

I didn't have more party duties, so I decided to use the leaf blower to clean the church sidewalks. It's something that needed to be done before church services on Sunday anyway. By the description of my life thus far, you may think I'm a janitor or even the church maintenance man. Actually, I guess that's true—I'm the unofficial church handyman, a jack-of-all-trades, but my official title is executive pastor.

As executive pastor, I'm the right-hand man to the senior lead pastor. I help him carry out the church's mission and take the reins on a lot of the day-to-day activities. I oversee organizational duties and church business to allow him to focus on the spiritual direction of our congregation and sermon development for weekly services.

I'm also the principal of the First Baptist Accelerated Academy, a thirty-student school for kindergarten through twelfth-grade students that operates on the church's campus. Our academy has a very specific purpose: to develop

I know how important it is to be a godly influence for young people.

world-changing ambassadors for Christ. I'm passionate about our mission. I know how important it is to be a godly influence for young people—to pour God's truth into them so they can go out and change the world. It's what I deeply want for each of the students and my own children. It's what I yearn for in my life as well.

Even though both my jobs are managerial, being able to repair things is one of my gifts. Everyone knows it. Once I was called to a fix-it job in our preschool area. There was a paper sign on the bathroom door: "Toilet is broken, Andrew is coming." Not a very spiritual image, but practical nonetheless. But it's more than that. People know I have a heart for helping. I've always been a hands-on guy—carpentry, appliance repair, any sort of troubleshooting when something won't work. I truly can fix most anything that's broken. But there was one problem I couldn't fix.

The past couple years had been stale. I'd never let myself say it out loud, but I felt as if I'd lost my passion for ministry. Stuck in a rut of never-ending busywork, I did church chores and implemented spiritual enrichment programs, and I always showed up with a smile. But deep inside my soul, the enthusiasm just wasn't there. I questioned myself. *Is my work making a difference? Am I making a difference?*

I had no intention of walking away from ministry, but I wondered if God intended more for me.

It's not as if I were bringing legions of people to Christ at our seventy-five-member church. Sure we had a few salvations with our youth and church members, maybe a handful or so each year. But wasn't there more I could be doing for the people of God? For those who were seeking the abundant life that Christ promised? I'm sad to say that I, too, was thirsty for that abundant life. My job felt more like a routine than a divine calling. Sometimes I felt like I was just going through the motions—same church calendar activities.

Because Natalie and I grew up in ministerial families, we were well acquainted with the ups and downs of a life in ministry. She got tired of seeing how much pastors worked and how the people they served just dismissed the extra time as a requirement of the job. It had taken a toll on her family when she was growing up as a pastor's kid.

I, too, saw how time-consuming it was for my dad and how it often pulled him away from our family because he was tending to so many different needs so often. Sometimes Mom and my brothers and I took a back seat to the requests of our church family.

Natalie and I tried to protect our relationship, our time, and our family, but people were so needy. It was not unusual for phone calls in the late evening to awaken our children or for me to talk to people calling with emergencies in the middle of the night. Natalie and I counseled them, prayed for them, and loved them. But it took its toll on us. On our family.

I realized that the same thing that had happened in our pastoral families growing up was now beginning to happen to us. And I had no idea how to fix it.

Often in the stillness of the night, I questioned myself. *Is this the path God meant for me?* I had no intention of walking away from ministry, but I couldn't help wondering if God intended more for me. I dreamed of doing big things when I was a young man—making a difference. I wanted to change the world. None of that was happening.

Still, growing in my faith was something very close to my heart. As a young person, I confirmed my commitment to serve the Lord through full-time ministry when I was influenced by two godly men at summer camp. Had it not been for that summer in 2000, I may not have found my way into ministry at all.

Called at Camp

Like every school, mine had cliques, but I had a strong core of friends. I didn't really have problems fitting in until high school, when I began to experience racism in the classroom and even on my high school sports teams. It wasn't uncommon for a few teammates to whisper racial slurs, using derogatory terms to refer to those of us who were of Mexican descent.

I was insecure but tried not to show it. Instead, I became a tough guy with a chip on my shoulder. Even though I was raised in the church, I pulled away from God my senior year. I started sneaking around and partying, longing to be accepted somewhere. Anywhere. I longed to fit in.

While in high school, I decided to pursue culinary arts. I wanted to find a career using my hands, and I liked cooking. I found a job as a cook at Hume Lake Christian Camp, about three hours east of Gilroy.

> *I longed to be accepted somewhere. Anywhere. I longed to fit in.*

High school graduation ceremonies conflicted with the first week of the camp session, so I started a few days after camp began. That put me at a disadvantage with the other employees who had gotten to know one another in the days before I arrived.

That first week, it was evident I didn't fit in. At all. A working-class Mexican kid from a low-income, high-crime neighborhood at a camp filled with mostly upper-class Caucasian students from privileged backgrounds. Suburbanites who didn't associate with people like me. And they let me know it. A few even hurled racial slurs to let me know they didn't want me around. I felt ignored and overlooked. I imagined they saw me like the kitchen help I was—someone who was only there to serve them. It felt like I was in high school all over again—on the outside looking in.

I hated the atmosphere and called Dad.

"Can you come pick me up? I want to go home." My voice quavered.

There was silence on the other end of the phone. My dad was old-school. He'd worked hard and held down two jobs his whole life. I pretty much knew what he would say.

"No, son. We're not coming to pick you up." His tone was gentle, but serious. "You have to give it at least two weeks."

I hung up the phone and walked slump-shouldered back to the cabin.

In the next few days, I met other employees who felt on the fringe too. They were not serious about their walk with Christ and ended up being a bad influence on me. A very small handful of people were there for the wrong reasons. And I hooked up with them.

Late one night, we snuck out of our cabins and met at someone's house. There was beer and a bottle of something harder. A couple of days went by. Word got out. The directors contacted us one by one over the next couple of days. Slowly but surely every person I was with that night got fired. Except me.

Did they know I was involved too? Living with the shame and guilt consumed me. The waiting was as hard as hearing the verdict. I knew it was just a matter of time until someone would find out, then I would be fired too.

I questioned myself. *What am I going to do with my life?* I knew what I did wasn't right, that I was on the wrong path. Sneaking around and partying wasn't what God intended for me; I was certain of that. But I was hurting inside. I wanted more. I simply didn't know how to get it.

Finally my day of reckoning arrived. Derek, one of the kitchen managers, found me in the kitchen cutting vegetables.

"You need to tell me what happened that night." He put a hand on my shoulder and gently pulled me back from the counter.

I'd been at Hume Lake and worked under Derek for about two weeks. He was in the kitchen with me and the other workers every day.

Our relationship had been purely professional. He only talked to me in regard to my kitchen duties. He directed me what to do, how to do it, and when to do it. We had never had a personal conversation or discussed anything deep. Until now.

"I don't know what you're talking about." Beads of perspiration formed on my forehead.

Derek took my elbow. We walked into the enormous dining room that was now vacant. I followed him to a table. He pulled out a chair at the end of the table and sat down. He nodded for me to sit in the chair next to him. My heart felt like it would beat out of my chest.

"I know you were involved." His tone was serious, but I saw a glimmer of empathy in his eyes. "You need to tell me what happened."

I bit the inside of my lip. Guilt and shame bubbled up. I was going to be fired. My voice trembled as I started to get honest. I really wanted to tell him what happened that night. I needed to get it over with.

As I talked, something inside me burst, like a dam when it's overfilled with water. I could no longer contain my emotions. I broke down. Sobs from the depth of my soul exploded from a lonely, scared place inside of me. I poured everything out to him, not just about the party that we had, but everything about my life spewed out of my mouth too. How I'd always felt excluded. The hurt, sadness, and frustration of the last fifteen years gushed out of me as he listened.

"I hate so much in myself. For years, I've felt like I didn't have much value and I was trying to cover it up. I used different things—first sports, then good grades, and then trying to be a cool kid with a bunch of tough friends. Last year, I turned to partying and getting drunk because

I was hurting inside. It's how I thought I could make myself feel like I fit in. But it never worked. Now, I want more. I don't want to live like that anymore."

I wiped my eyes and stared at him. I had nothing else to say. I was guilty. I deserved to be fired like everyone else that I snuck out with that night.

Derek was quiet for a moment.

A sinking feeling formed in my stomach. *I'm getting fired. I'm about to be sent back home for the summer. Why did I do something so stupid? What will my parents say? How can I live with myself knowing I've disgraced myself and my family so much?*

Derek pushed back from the table a bit. He crossed his ankle over his knee and sighed.

As I talked, something inside me burst, like a dam.

"We need to talk to Brian." Brian was the director of the food service program. "You need to be here more than I do. If Brian wants to fire you, I'm going to ask him to fire me instead and let you stay."

I looked at him incredulously. No one had ever done something like that for me. Especially a white man who had authority over me. His radical idea surely would not be accepted. Just then I looked up. About fifteen feet away, Brian stood in the doorway. His footsteps echoed through the cavernous dining hall as he approached our table. I swallowed hard and wiped my eyes.

Coming straight toward me, he kept his gaze on mine.

He stood beside my chair. "Why?" He lifted his hands and cocked his head.

I'd just cried my guts out with Derek, so my feelings were still close to the surface. Guilt and shame poured out of me in a deluge of uncontrollable sobs. I confessed. I told him everything—what had happened that night and that I made such a wrong decision all because I hoped to be liked and included.

When I was finished talking, Derek spoke.

"If you want to fire him, Brian, please take my job. Fire me in his place," he said with sincerity. "I have a real sense that Andrew needs to be here—that God wants him to stay."

Their acts of grace cracked my frozen heart. I was able to let God in.

Brian crossed his arms. He studied Derek's face. I watched his gaze fall on me, as if he was processing and weighing all the options. I had no idea what would happen.

"Okay, you're forgiven," Brian said softly, slowly.

I was able to stay and work at Hume Lake Christian Camp that summer and so was Derek. But his unselfish offer and the act of being forgiven for something I was guilty of changed everything for me. It opened my eyes to deeply understand the good news that I'd heard from the pulpit my whole life. *Jesus died for us. Not only us, but for me. Even though I didn't deserve it. The sinless Son of God died for our sins. For my sins.*

Brian and Derek manifested the gospel to me. Derek put his job on the line. When he didn't deserve to be punished, he was willing to take my punishment. Brian forgave me for what I was guilty of—for what I deserved to be fired for. Somehow, their acts of grace cracked my frozen heart. I was able to let God in.

Through working in the kitchen that summer, I grew in my relationship with and love for the Lord. I started reading my Bible. I took notes when the speakers preached in the chapel sessions. I started to worship freely through memorizing Scripture, singing, and talking with others.

When negative things happened to me, I would count them as blessings. I sensed deep in my spirit that God had more for me. And I wanted to serve Him through ministry. I wasn't insignificant to God. I wanted to do something big for Him. I wanted to make a difference for the kingdom of heaven. I wanted to change the world.

I stayed on at Camp Hume for another year, then continued with an intensive nine-month discipleship training program. My love of God was real. I knew I wanted to serve Him.

Devastating Accident

Back at my church, I put my arms through the leaf blower straps and made my way to the sidewalk, listening to the blower hum as I shimmied it back and forth to clear the twigs and leaves. I recalled Scripture from Ecclesiastes 9:10 (NASB): "Whatever your hand finds to do, do it with all your might." I was happiest when I could use my hands. This was ministry too. My favorite kind of service—to God and to others.

The bright spot in my life was our little family. Natalie and I had been married for seven years. Cara and Corban were our world—the light of our lives. Our two beautiful gifts from God. That's what today was about. Celebrating Cara. Focusing on my family, on my daughter's birthday party.

But there were regular weekly chores I needed to do to get ready for Sunday morning services. And I had an hour to spare, after all. I usually got the church ready for Sunday morning on Saturday anyway. *Might as well get it out of the way now.*

My movements seemed to happen in slow motion as I fell backward.

With the nozzle pointed downward, I watched twigs, leaves, and debris fly up and scatter off the walkways. There was something satisfying about the action, that with a whisk of wind I could eliminate the remains of last night's storm. *If only I could clean up the emotional messes of life this easily.* As if with a puff of wind, all my cares would fly away and disappear into the landscape.

I'd been cleaning up the sidewalks for about twenty minutes. I walked around the corner of the education building and onto a slight downward slope, just behind the main church sanctuary, leaf nozzle in hand. I blew debris out of the four-foot-wide flower beds that hugged the stucco exterior.

I stepped backward to get an area I'd missed. I felt the garden edger underneath my shoe, which made me unsteady. The ten-pound weight of the leaf blower on my back unbalanced me. I fell backward. Toward the building.

My movements seemed to happen in slow motion, though I was fully aware that what was happening was taking place in actual time too. I reached my left arm out straight, toward the structure, hoping to put my hand on the building and catch myself from falling. Instead of landing on the stucco exterior, my fingers hit a full-length, single-pane glass window there. By the time I realized that I was falling onto the window, it was too late.

My hand hit the cool, glass surface. There was no way it could hold me. No way could it steady my balance. I felt the glass flex inward. I knew it was going to break. And that my arm was going to slam clear through it.

Crash!

The window shattered. My left arm fell forcefully on top of the jagged glass that remained on the bottom of the pane.

I watched in speechless horror as my arm was sliced to pieces by the sharp edges. Shards fell like raindrops, shattering on the ground. I looked at my arm. Disbelief mixed with terror. My stomach turned queasy. *God, help me!*

My arm was sliced all the way around the elbow joint. Blood gushed down to my wrist. Muscles, tendons, and chunks of flesh hung out of my bicep. The bones were still attached, but everything else was severed.

"Help! Help! Help!" My voice was so shrill that it startled me. I fell to my knees and toppled to the ground.

The CPR certification training I had every two years at the school kicked in. I knew the first step in any emergency was always to get help.

I jumped up. I was hidden here alone, behind the building. No one else was around. I needed to get out in the open, to run toward the street. Hopefully a car would drive by. Someone would see me and stop.

Blood stained the ground around me. My blood.

"Help! Help! Help!"

I grabbed my injured arm with my right hand and squeezed my flesh just above the nearly amputated elbow. Blood shot out of it. A terrifying thought pushed its way to the front of my mind. *I'm going to die!*

"Help me! Help!"

I've got to find help! I ran toward the back parking lot, but my knees were weak. A few seconds after the accident, and I was already fighting dizziness. The rush of adrenaline was the only thing keeping me moving.

The world was spinning fast. Blood gushed from my arm.

If I could flag down a car.

"Help me! Someone help!" I screamed as I ran, holding my arm high in the air in an attempt to slow the bleeding.

Suddenly the world was spinning fast. Disoriented, I knew I was losing consciousness. Blood gushed from my arm like water from an opened fire hydrant on a hot summer day.

After a few seconds, I made it to the back of the parking lot, now in view of someone who might pass by on the street. My right hand fell to my side. I reached into my front pocket. I fished out my cell phone and dialed 911.

"I just cut off my arm!" I yelled to the dispatcher. "I need help! I'm dying!"

No longer could I run. Everything blurred.

She asked my location. Amazingly, I remembered the church address.

"Can you wrap a towel around it to make a tourniquet?" she said.

My vision was cloudy. The earth seemed to wobble around me. I saw movement up ahead. A tall, blond, skinny guy. He was running, looking from side to side. As if searching for something. *Searching for me?*

He spotted me and stopped, then ran faster in my direction. I felt light-headed, as if I was about to pass out. The blond guy came up to me. He was young—maybe a teen—I couldn't tell how old. Our eyes met. His face turned ashen. I saw terror in his eyes. I handed him my phone.

Dizziness overtook me. I bent at the waist. *I'm going to pass out.* I squatted to get my bearings. I knew I needed to lie down. I hit the ground. I lay back onto the parking lot pavement.

The world began to dim. A desperate prayer formed on my lips: *Please, God! Don't let me die! Please, save me! I need to be here for my wife and kids...I need to be here for my wife and kids...I need...*

Everything turned dark.

Big Screen, Little Moments

Immediately I saw myself, my body lying on the ground on the church parking lot. But my point of view wasn't from within my body. I seemed to see myself from a higher vantage point. I hovered in the air as I looked down on the scene that was taking place below. Injured, bleeding, near death. I saw myself lying on the concrete parking lot. *Is this a vision?* The line between realities blurred.

In the time it takes to snap my fingers, the image of my body disappeared. Everything became black.

Then the blackness gave way to light. As if someone steadily pushed up the dimmer switch, the darkness was quickly erased by a bright, white light. I felt somewhat conscious but wasn't able to see or hear what was going on around me The light was the whitest I'd ever seen, but it didn't hurt my eyes as it should have.

Time seemed to stop. All I felt was peace. Extreme tranquility washed over me. I was composed and serene, basking in this white light. No longer was I lying injured on earth. My arm wasn't even cut. I felt no pain, no fear. I was whole, standing and surrounded by this great white light. What a difference from the panic and terror I felt moments earlier.

I didn't try to speak or even think. I tried to make sense of my surroundings. I looked around and couldn't see anyone else—I was totally alone, and yet at the same time, I felt a presence in this great white light. I somehow knew it was the presence of God. I knew God was there with me, even though I saw no one and had the impression that I was alone. Perhaps God was not so much *in* the great white light. Perhaps He *was* the light.

Before I could figure out what was happening or where I was, a huge screen appeared in the distance, maybe thirty feet away. It filled my sight. Out of my peripheral vision I sensed it encircling me—this giant, 360-degree, wraparound movie screen that looked to be four stories high, at least forty feet tall. And I stood in the very center of it.

On the screen were thousands of tiny squares. Each square featured an image. Each image reminded me of an activity, frozen in time as if it were a still photograph. There were so many squares that I couldn't take the time to look at each one, but I knew they weren't photographs. I intuitively knew that they were moments. Moments from my life. People I'd met. People I was close to. People I'd had a relationship with. My friends and family. They were all represented in these pictures. I saw experiences in the images too. Things I'd done in my lifetime.

Events both minor and important. Every incident I'd experienced was accounted for.

Somehow I understood. The story of my life was being played out before me on thousands of these small squares. I didn't recognize what every square was, exactly, but they were all positive. All happy. All beautiful. My life was all around me on this enormous movie screen. I stood as still as a statue, surrounded by it all, soaking it in. An overwhelming sense of joy flooded over me.

Time seemed to stop. All I felt was peace.

My attention zeroed in on a few of the images. Natalie. Our kids, Cara and Corban. They smiled at me from their spot on the screen. Then, as if being summoned one by one, a square that seemed tiny in the distance flew off the screen and hovered close to my face. It blocked my view of anything else with its presence.

The first was Natalie. Her smile, her eyes as soft as velvet. The poster-sized picture of my beautiful wife filled my vision. I could almost reach out and touch her. She seemed just an arm's length away. As soon as Natalie came close, she just as quickly zoomed away, back to her place on the distant screen.

Before I had a chance to miss her, an image of Cara whizzed forward toward me. My firstborn. My precious daughter, who was once far away on the distant screen, came near me in the identical way Natalie had. She flitted close to my face, her sweet appearance so close that I could imagine her saying, "Hi, Daddy," before she disappeared to join the others back on the screen.

Nanoseconds later, the image of Corban shot to the forefront like a rocket. He grinned in his impish, childlike way. His giggle erupted in my memory.

One after the other, different images of my family paraded in front of my face.

One by one, over and over again, the three of them took turns coming close to me in different individual pictures. They flew off the screen and hovered directly in front of my face so that I could see nothing else except their beautiful portraits. Different images, but very similar too—each just a headshot of a lovely, smiling face. Boom. Boom. Boom. One after the other, maybe fifteen or twenty different images of my beloved Natalie, Cara, and Corban paraded in front of my face. All smiling. All happy. The emotion of love consumed me.

Seeing my life story in pictures and experiencing my family reiterated to me what I truly valued in life. My family. My wife and kids. They were my ministry, my purpose, my calling. My reason for living.

Overwhelming love covered me. The love I had for them. The love they had for me.

The three of them were illuminated by something in those pictures, a kind of light. Like halos of love. Love for me. Love that I knew came from God. He was the source of all the love I'd given them multiplied with all the love I'd received over the past thirty-four years of my life.

How could I have ever taken even one moment of my life for granted? Every event was precious. Every interaction priceless. My beautiful life.

As quickly as it had come, the screen disappeared. The light got even brighter, a brighter white, an empty space. It was so quiet—more silent than anything I'd ever experienced. At that moment, I knew that my life was over. I don't know how to explain it, but I knew deep in my soul that I was about to pass on. *This is it. I'm dying.*

I was not worried. I was not scared. Even though I knew I was dying, I knew the Spirit of God was with me, present in the great white light. I was in the presence of God. Peacefulness enveloped me.

A Painful Return

W*hoosh!*

I heaved a giant breath, sucking in deeply. My chest lifted off the ground, kind of like in the movies when the patient's heart stops and the doctor revives him with paddles. I was back, lying on the pavement of the church parking lot. I inhaled a second breath. I felt as though life had been poured back into my body. Like someone had captured my runaway soul and shoved it back up inside me, waking me out of death and back into life. With that second deep breath, I opened my eyes. I could see again. See what was happening around me—see what was happening to me.

Two paramedics knelt over me. One cut away my shirt. The other tightened the tourniquet on my arm. The blond stranger, tears streaming down his cheeks, stood with a couple of passersby, their brows furrowed with concern. Out of the corner of my eye, I watched a woman running toward me. I'm not sure if she spied my mangled arm or saw my trail of blood, but whatever it was made her double over. She threw up in the parking lot.

Just then Natalie's mom walked around the corner with a bunch of balloons for Cara's birthday party.

"Noooooo," she shouted. "Andrew!"

A firefighter blocked her from coming close to me.

"It's okay, Shari," I yelled. "I cut off my arm."

With the tightening of the tourniquet, I was fully back.

I'm not sure if she heard me or not. She was screaming frantically and crying. I knew she'd alert Natalie.

With the tightening of the tourniquet, I was fully back. Instantly conscious again. Alive. And in really, really intense, unbearable pain. More horrific than anything I'd ever felt or imagined.

Paramedics slid a stretcher underneath me and lifted. As they quickly carried me to the ambulance, each step they took sent thousands of knifelike pricks searing through my body.

"This hurts so bad. This hurts so bad." I screamed like it was a mantra that I couldn't stop reciting. Inside the back of the ambulance, it was even worse as the tires bumped and dipped down the street.

I groaned in anguish.

The paramedic fiddled with medical-looking items inside the shelves of the ambulance's interior.

"Am I gonna die?" I squeezed my eyes tight.

Silence.

I screamed in agony and moaned.

"This hurts so bad! So bad! Am I going to die?"

"We're just trying to stop the bleeding," he answered without making eye contact, as he treated my arm above the tourniquet.

I screamed. "It hurts! It hurts!"

He wouldn't give me any reassurance. And I desperately needed some reassurance because I didn't think that anyone could have this excruciating level of pain and still survive.

"Am I gonna die? You've got to tell me! Am I going to die?"

"No, you're not going to die," he whispered matter-of-factly as he looked into my eyes. "You're not going to die."

He was a young guy, maybe younger than me. He may not have even known what he was talking about, but when I heard his answer, something switched inside me.

I exhaled. *I'm not going to die.* His opinion, whether valid or not, gave me the hope I needed. I was still in intense pain, but his affirmative words built a confidence that I was going to make it. I looked upward, then squeezed my eyes tight.

I might lose my arm, but I'm going to live. It didn't matter. I just didn't want to die. Then I remembered my prayer. The prayer I prayed right before I blacked out—praying that God would let me live. *God, You answered my prayer! God, You answered my prayer! Thank You! Thank You for not letting me die!*

Within five minutes, the ambulance arrived at the emergency department at Los Robles Hospital & Medical Center.

Looking Back: Coincidence or God-Incidence?

The rest of the day unfolded in a series of coincidences—or were they God-incidences? One of California's most skilled plastic surgeons, Kouros Azar, MD, a Westlake Village–based, board-certified plastic and reconstructive surgeon, happened to be on call at the hospital that day. A plastic surgeon by specialty, Dr. Azar has experience in reattaching fingers and limbs as well as complex reconstruction cases, which uniquely qualified him to treat Andrew's devastating injury.

The day unfolded in a series of coincidences— or were they God-incidences?

Andrew had severed his median nerve, which controls the muscles in the fingers, and sliced through blood vessels, veins, and arteries. He cut all the muscles and tendons as well.

"It's like killing both the computer in your car and the engine," Dr. Azar explained. "You need an engine to make the car move, but you also need a computer to control the engine."

It took seven hours of surgery using countless stitches, but Dr. Azar performed the reattachment of the arm, as well as the nerves, muscles, arteries, and tendons. Andrew underwent three blood transfusions during the complex procedure.

Andrew spent the next six days in the hospital's intensive-care unit. Dr. Azar monitored his patient's progress by looking in on him several times a day.

It wasn't the first time Dr. Azar had reattached an arm. More than a decade earlier, he reattached the left arm of a man who had been cut by a twenty-two-inch propeller on a radio-controlled model airplane. The arm had been 80 percent detached at the elbow.

Interestingly enough, Dr. Azar was the only doctor around who had any sort of experience in an injury like this. He admitted that the procedure "required a certain experience and attention to detail that not everybody had."

Dr. Azar just happened to be the one on call at the hospital when Andrew arrived.

And what about the blond guy who spotted Andrew in the church parking lot? His name is Zach Taylor, a twenty-year-old college student. Andrew handed him his phone before he passed out. Zach talked to the 911 dispatcher as Andrew lost consciousness. The dispatcher urged him to get a towel, so he sprinted home and returned with a towel to hold against Andrew's arm. Medical officials predicted that if Zach hadn't done that, Andrew would've died within a minute.

Zach ran so fast that he surprised himself. Months after Andrew's accident, he signed up to do his first marathon. Zach continues to run as a hobby now.

The first responders arrived within three minutes of the phone call. If they hadn't gotten there so quickly, and Andrew had bled for another thirty seconds or so, they believed that he would not have been able to be resuscitated.

Exactly what brought Zach to Andrew's side? He wasn't a member of First Baptist Church, Thousand Oaks. He didn't come running until he heard screams and saw Andrew was injured. He'd simply left his house at the exact time Andrew needed help. Zach had wandered onto the church grounds to look for his cat that he noticed was missing moments earlier. Instead, he found a dying man who had almost sliced off his arm.

Natalie's View

Sirens wailed down the street that Saturday morning. I sat cross-legged in front of Corban's closet mirror door, putting on my makeup. Cara was twirling and whirling in her room, excited for her big day. It was late morning, and we were getting dressed and ready to go to her birthday party. Andrew had gotten up bright and early to meet the bounce house guy for the party.

I was supposed to have been up and ready with the kids by now. When Andrew came home from setting up the bounce house, we needed to get Cara's piñata and head to the party. But when Andrew returned, I wasn't ready. To give me more time, he decided to go over to the church to do some normal Saturday prep duties for our Sunday morning service.

The sirens got louder and louder, and they didn't fade.

The kids and I heard first one siren and then another. It's not uncommon to hear sirens since we live at a busy intersection, and the fire department is about a mile down the road. The sirens got louder and louder. Usually we heard them fade as they raced through the inter-section. But these didn't fade.

Cara, Corban, and I hopped up to look out the window and catch a glimpse. We saw the fire engine and ambulance turn to go along the side of our church and up the road. When they were out of sight, I told the kids they must be headed to a neighbor's house.

"We should say a prayer," I said.

I grabbed their hands, we bowed our heads, and I prayed. Then I continued getting ready and getting the kids dressed, brushing hair and locating shoes.

What happened in these next few moments will haunt me the rest of my life. And it would be the beginning of a terrifying, miraculous, painful, hope-filled journey for our family.

Mom opened the front door and called my name. It was strange she would call my name from downstairs. Her voice sounded thick, afraid. Just by the way my mother said my name, I knew something horrible had happened.

I hurried down the stairs. I rounded the landing and saw her face as she stood in the wide-open front door. I knew something terrible had happened.

My legs buckled beneath me.

"It's Andrew," she whispered, her voice trembling, hands shaking.

I knew nothing, but I knew it must be bad. Really bad.

Dad rushed through the open door. He put an arm around me to help me to my feet. "We need to go. We need to go, now."

I scrambled up the stairs on my hands and knees, my body like jelly. Cara and Corban stood in the bedroom crying, confused and scared. I hugged them hard, kissed them, and said it was going to be okay. Mom came upstairs to comfort them as I raced down.

Dad quickly helped me into his car. We sped off to the hospital about two miles away. I kept asking Dad what happened. All he knew was that Andrew had fallen through a plate-glass window while using a leaf blower.

It was the longest ride of my life. My dad prayed aloud in the car, pleading the blood of Jesus over Andrew. My body shook. I cried and repeated "Jesus" over and over and over and over.

We pulled into the emergency entrance. I jumped out of the car before it stopped. I ran in and truly could not say the words to speak a clear sentence.

"My husband, my husband," I cried as I ran to the triage desk. A nurse met me.

"He just arrived a couple minutes ago. They're working on him," she said gravely.

Dad rushed in. I was already in shock. I couldn't think what I was supposed to do. My mouth was like cotton. Sweat poured down my back. Someone handed me a cup of water. I sipped it, then raced to the bathroom and vomited.

When I came out, a nurse met me at the door.

"Andrew is conscious," she said slowly, making sure I understood. "He needs you, but I have to warn you. His injury is severe. If you go in, you have to hold it together. He needs you to be strong. I'm worried you won't be able to."

I promised her I could handle it. I promised I'd hold myself together.

She escorted me back. The moment the door opened, I heard Andrew's screams. Deep groaning, high-pitched gasping, and agonizing screams. I won't forget those gut-wrenching sounds for as long as I live.

Andrew lay there with a folded sheet over him. There were so many people. Rushing. Moving around him. I walked straight toward him and cupped his face in my hands.

Then I saw his arm. I couldn't make sense of it. What was I looking at? *Oh, dear Jesus!* It was beyond terrifying. His bicep was exposed, balled up high on his arm. Purple and red, it had severed and snapped like a rubber band under tension. Everything else was just a mess of tissue, tendon, and exposed bone. His left arm, left hand, was hanging. Severed three-fourths of the way, his left arm was only being held on by some skin tissue and elbow bone.

I made sure I didn't look at it again.

The tourniquet that was placed on his arm caused him indescribable pain. Andrew screamed in agony. Blood was everywhere. I started praying in my mind, nothing eloquent. *Please save him! Don't let him die!*

I'd never seen an injury like that—even in the goriest horror movie. I didn't know how anyone could live through it. I willed myself not to go there. To be strong, to hold it together. I needed Andrew to know he would get through this.

> *I willed myself to be strong, to hold it together.*

He wasn't crying, but tears rolled down his face. I talked calmly in his ear. He kept saying over and over that he was sorry. That he didn't want to die. I begged the doctors to give him something to make his pain stop.

I tried to reassure him. Tried to reassure myself. It was the hardest thing I'd ever done.

The ER techs said there was nothing more that could be done until he was in the operating room.

We waited for the surgeons on call to arrive. The vascular surgeon was riding his mountain bike on a trail about fifteen minutes away. The supervising OR doc hopped in her car and picked him up, bike and all.

Meanwhile in the ER, they worked on keeping Andrew alive. He was going into shock. They estimated he had lost approximately four liters of blood.

An hour passed. The surgeons were ready. I kissed his cold, tear-stained face.

"I love you," I said, not knowing if I'd ever kiss my husband again.

Two orderlies wheeled him away to the operating room. I followed them as far as they'd let me. Then the doors closed.

A nurse handed me a bag of his belongings and his bloodstained shoes. I couldn't hold on to them and asked my dad to throw them away. He handed me the bag with Andrew's wedding ring and took the other belongings away from me.

I fell to my knees. Sobbing, I prayed.

All my strength had been used to hold back my emotions while I was in the presence of my husband. Now I could barely hold back my sobs. I couldn't think straight. I was alone. And desperate.

I tried to find the surgery waiting room but couldn't. Instead, I found a chair in a nearby waiting area. I walked toward the chair, but halfway there I fell to my knees. I knelt, sobbing while I prayed. Deep wails erupted from my soul.

"Please, God. Please." I didn't need to finish my prayer. God knew I was begging for the life of my husband to be spared.

In that moment the battle was real.

Before long I felt a tap on my shoulder. It was a nurse.

"I'm glad I found you," she said. "I want to help you understand what is happening."

After answering lots of random questions, she assured me that even if Andrew lost his arm, they were doing everything they could to save his life.

It wasn't long before I looked up and saw familiar faces. First, a friend from church. I was still crying. He silently put his hand on my back. Then another friend arrived. And another and another until the waiting room was filled with family, friends, and church members sitting on the floor praying with me.

For seven hours and thirty minutes we waged war as only Christians do. We petitioned heaven, praying, begging, and crying. My friends helped me to drink some water and eat some grapes. Some other friends went to the house and took Cara and Corbin across the street. These moms put my children first and hosted Cara's birthday party. They did the best they could for my kids. For our family. For me.

I desperately needed the body of Christ then and would continue to rely on it for many months to come.

My uncle and aunt arrived at the house by evening. They took the kids to McDonald's and let them play at the playground at church so Mom could join me at the hospital.

At about 9:30 p.m. the surgeon came out. They had saved Andrew's life and reattached his arm. But Andrew was in a tough place. He had lost much blood. The surgery had been long and difficult. We didn't know if the attachment would take. And infection would now be his greatest enemy.

I walked into the recovery room where my husband lay. They kept the room at 90 degrees Fahrenheit to promote blood flow to his arm. His eyes opened and met mine. We both knew our lives would never be the same.

Andrew's Recuperation and New Life

After being admitted through the emergency department and having surgery, I was transferred to the hospital's intensive-care unit. My left arm was three times the size of my right with the swelling, gauze wrap, and medical brace. It rested in a sling that kept it bent at the elbow and close to my chest. My third day in ICU, Dr. Azar pulled a chair next to the left side of my bed.

Little did I know then that nine surgeries and procedures were in store for me.

He asked how I was feeling and wanted me to talk about my pain level. He was a serious yet kind man. I could tell that he really cared about my recovery, my well-being. I admired his medical expertise and was exceedingly grateful to him, knowing that he had basically saved my life. Then Dr. Azar said something that stumped me.

"We're going to tighten your laces today," he said in his calm, low tone.

Tighten my laces? I had no idea what he was talking about. I watched as he removed the sling from around my neck and gently placed my arm down on the bed. Using surgical scissors, he cut through the tape and unwrapped the layers of gauze to expose the long, twelve-inch open wound that ran from just above my wrist all the way up to my bicep.

I gulped hard and stared wide-eyed at my opened flesh. The four-inch-wide area of red muscles and tendons was a startling contrast to my skin tone beneath the crisscrossed white plastic-lace sutures. Dr. Azar explained that the lace that was looped through metal staples attached on my flesh would slowly move my skin back into place. It worked on the same premise as a shoelace. He would tighten the laces by gradually pulling the end taut. Thanks to the heavy pain medication, I didn't feel it at all, but the sight of the monstrous gash overwhelmed me. Sure, I knew I had a life-threatening injury, but somehow with my arm bundled up and resting against my chest, the knowledge was easier to deal with than what I was seeing now—the huge open slash that looked like something out of a horror film. *Dear God, how am I going to get through this?*

Dr. Azar explained that injuries of this magnitude were left open to account for the massive swelling and to make sure the muscles, nerves, and tendons were healing correctly before the next surgery. *Another surgery?* Little did I know then that nine surgeries and procedures were in store for me, as well as a lifetime of therapies to care for my injured arm.

My ICU room was a bustle of activity. Doctors, nurses, and technicians came to my bedside at all hours to check my vitals, administer pain medication, and change my surgical dressing. There was so much going on around me that my mind couldn't rest. I really didn't process what had happened to me or, more importantly, what was going to happen to me. There was always something to distract me from going deep with my thoughts.

That changed after six days in the ICU. I was moved to a regular patient room on the third floor. I was by myself. Alone with my life-changing injury and an incredible level of pain. Alone with lots of time to think.

I desperately missed my kids. Children weren't allowed in the ICU, so it had been almost a week since I'd seen Cara and Corban. But hospitals can be scary places. The echoing hallways. Medical staff wearing scrubs, masks, and gloves. If the kids came up, I worried about how they would react to the odd sights and smells. I was relegated to a bed and hooked up to medical equipment. Would the bandages on my arm frighten them? More importantly, would I?

As deep as my concern was for their reaction, deeper still was my longing to see them. I talked to Natalie. She agreed she'd bring the kids once I was settled in my hospital room.

My beloved family. Joy swept over me.

The next day, I turned my head to see a trio of silhouettes paused in the doorway. My beloved family. Joy swept over me. I was so happy that I think I might have chuckled.

"Hi, Daddy!" Cara called. A big smile spread across her face. She looked up at Natalie for permission.

"It's okay," Natalie encouraged her. "Go ahead."

I held out my right arm. Cara hurried to my bedside. I gave her a squeeze with my good arm.

"Look," she said. She held up a stuffed frog that had a bandage on its front leg.

Natalie and Corban waited behind Cara. I noticed hesitation in Corban's eyes.

"Hey, buddy." I reached my hand out to Corban. He grinned and scooted next to Cara. I hugged them both close.

Natalie helped them climb up on the bed next to my right side.

"Be gentle and sit still," she warned.

"Is it okay, Daddy? Are we hurting you?" Cara asked.

They might have been worried about harming me in some way, but I wasn't. Just having my family here chased away the dark feelings—the "what-ifs." Of course, I was still on powerful painkillers and sleepy. They stayed for about twenty minutes before I felt my eyelids get heavy.

"Daddy needs to rest," announced Natalie. "Give him a kiss."

They left and I drifted off, more content than I'd been all week.

An Emotional Roller Coaster

Day after day, I lay on my back in a hospital bed waiting for my arm to heal. I drifted in and out of sleep. When I was awake, I had a lot of time to think. Too much time.

I stared at the ceiling as the television hummed in the background. *What's going to happen to me?* The bandages on my arm were sort of a blessing, because I could deny the gravity of my injury that was hidden underneath. However, reality set in each time the nurse unwrapped the gauze to change the dressing or Dr. Azar came in to assess my progress and my once strong, healthy arm. *Will I ever be able to use it again? To what extent? Will I always be in this much pain?*

Fear, doubt, and insecurity flooded my mind. Prior to my accident, I was the guy people called when they needed something fixed. But what good was a one-arm handyman? I couldn't help but question my value and my worth. Not just on the job, but at home too. Would Natalie grow tired of waiting on me as I rehabilitated? Would I be able to lift my kids high in the air as I did with Cara the morning of her birthday party? Would I be able to teach Corban to play baseball—to hold the bat? To catch and throw the ball?

In my head I knew I was a child of God and that my identity wasn't found in any of those things. What I could do, or couldn't do, was irrelevant. But I couldn't help feeling scared that people wouldn't love me anymore. I was afraid that my wife and children would lose a part of their love for me because I was no longer the man I once was. Every relationship that I could think of ultimately came down to this: *Will God still be able to use me now that I'm a broken man?*

Knock, knock, knock. I looked over at the door. *Natalie.* My parents stood behind her. I quickly wiped my eyes.

I don't know how anyone can love me anymore, I said.

They filed through the doorway, Natalie first, followed by Mom and Dad. Natalie came to the right side of the bed.

"Hi, babe," she whispered, stroking the hair off my forehead. She bent down and kissed me on the cheek. I wondered if she tasted my salty tears from earlier.

"How are you feeling, son?" Dad asked.

I talked about the intense pain I had in my arm. I talked about how the medication made me feel nauseated, sleepy, and loopy. I tried to make a joke about how tired I was of Jell-O and hospital food. But besides being my father, Dad was also a licensed counselor. I knew what he was really asking, but I just didn't want to go there and awaken those emotions.

Dad stood near the foot of the bed. He put his hand on my shin.

"How are you feeling, emotionally?"

Immediately tears welled up. There was no stopping them.

"I don't know how anyone can love me anymore," I started. "I won't ever be the same. Nothing will be the same. I'll be a burden to Natalie..."

Natalie slid her hand into my right hand and squeezed tightly. Her dark eyes radiated compassion.

"Why did God let me live if I can't do anything anymore? I just keep thinking that it might have been better if I died."

"Andrew, why do you feel this way?" Dad asked softly.

"I'm the one who takes care of things. I'm supposed to take care of others—Natalie, the kids, the church, the school, the congregation. But now..."

My tears flowed freely. I squeezed my eyes shut, hoping to hold back my tears, as well as some of my painful feelings.

"I'm the one they call when they need help. Now I can't do anything. I can't help anyone. I can't even hold my kids. They can't touch me. I can't play with them..."

Everyone was silent. I thought they were just letting me have a good cry until I heard Mom sniff. I opened my eyes. They were crying too. Crying with me.

I'll never forget what Dad said next. "You know, Andrew, it's not the things that you do for people that causes them to love you. It's the intention behind the action. Your intentions. People love you, not for what you do for them, but because of who you are. They love you because of your heart."

I thought about his words. Of course the people in my life were not so shallow that they loved me only for what I could do for them. I knew that was true.

Knock, knock, knock.

Natalie's parents, Shari and Jack, stood at the door. Shari held a potted plant.

I wiped my eyes, took in a deep breath, and looked at my family. I was surrounded by people who loved me. Under the most logical circumstances, I should have bled to death. But God had saved my life. I was still here for a reason. I would get through this—we would get through this, together, with the support of God, and with my family by my side. God wasn't finished with me yet. He still had more for me to do. He had a plan for me and for my life. I just needed to determine what it was and how I could accomplish it.

A Lifetime of Recovery

After ten days, I came home from the hospital. I had to pass several discharge tests in order to be released. I needed to be able to stand, walk, and climb stairs on my own. I was barely able to do those activities. I was still incredibly weak and had excruciating pain. It would take months of exercise and physical therapy for me to regain the strength I needed to perform everyday activities.

The same thoughts of inadequacy and insecurity that plagued me in the hospital lingered.

Natalie drove me home from the hospital that Tuesday afternoon. She pulled in front of our house and met me in front of the passenger-side door. I still was not stable and could only walk short distances. Natalie slid her arm around my waist. *I was the one who usually helped her. How long would our roles be reversed?* I pushed down my pride as we slowly walked to the porch.

Shari was watching Corban, and Cara was still at school. Inside I saw two homemade, hand-colored, construction paper signs with "Welcome Home, Daddy" colored with crayons. A stack of cards from friends and our church family, a couple of floral arrangements, and a balloon bouquet waited for me on the kitchen table. But most notable was the large, brand-new electronic reclining chair that sat in the middle of our living room.

The medical staff at the hospital advised Natalie to get the high-dollar chair since I couldn't lie flat while my injury healed. I needed the lift feature so I wouldn't be tempted to use my left arm while getting up and down. Dr. Azar also recommended that I not make a habit of climbing stairs for a while, and our bedroom was upstairs. So this would be my recovery chair.

It was only forty feet from the car to the living room, but exerting that energy exhausted me. Natalie showed me how to use the controls on the chair. I let it rise to meet me. I sat down gingerly into the comfortable seat. Within minutes, I was asleep.

In the months that followed, Natalie drove me to doctor and physical therapy appointments, usually five to seven times a week. She fixed all my meals, helped me get dressed and undressed, and even had to help me bathe. It was very humbling.

The same thoughts of inadequacy and insecurity that plagued me in the hospital lingered in the corners of my mind. I loathed that I put this hardship on Natalie and my family. But not just my family. My responsibilities at work were divided among the other staff. A substitute teacher covered for me in the classroom. One of my volunteer youth leaders jumped in and started leading the church youth group. My in-laws took the kids a lot. So many people's lives were turned upside down.

I tried to busy my mind. I didn't want to think. I tried to read my Bible. Tried to pray. But I felt far from God. Far from everyone, including myself. Depression and anxiety were my closest companions.

One morning after I'd been home a few weeks, I just couldn't take it anymore. I broke down. Negative thoughts overwhelmed me—the same thoughts I'd had so many times before. *I'm not good enough. I'm not worthy. No one will love me.* I began to shake and cry uncontrollably.

> *Depression and anxiety were my closest companions.*

Natalie was alarmed when she found me hunched over in the chair. "Babe, what's wrong?"

I told her my insecurities. My fears.

"Those things are not true!" She wrapped her arms around my neck and looked at my face with her velvet-soft eyes. "I love you. The kids love you. Everyone is praying for you. We'll get through this together."

By this time, tears were running down her cheeks too.

"Andrew, God has great things for you. That has never changed. You just had an accident. You have to believe me."

For the next six months, friends, church members, and coworkers stopped by to say hello. Sometimes they brought gifts, desserts, or a meal. Coworkers picked up the slack at the school and at church. My cell phone rang several times a day with calls and texts from people who wanted me to know they were thinking of me. Students at our school periodically sent handmade cards and letters of encouragement. I was on the First Baptist Church Thousand Oak's prayer chain with people praying around the clock. My extended family—parents, brothers, aunts, uncles, and cousins—had put me on prayer chains as well. So many people rallied around us, praying for us daily and sending us encouraging messages.

Still, I struggled with doubts. Hopelessness swirled around my soul, like a wave that formed out in the ocean, building and breaking as it rushed to the shore. I started seeing a professional counselor to help me in my struggle with self-worth.

On top of my despair over my emotional state, bills began to flood in. There were a lot of expenses that insurance was not going to cover. Like many in ministry, we lived paycheck to paycheck. Thankfully, I would get workman's comp while I was on leave, but that wasn't a full paycheck. We had additional costs, like my super-expensive recliner and converting our bathroom and bathtub to be handicapped friendly.

Always practical, my father brought up the issue of finances. He approached me about starting a GoFundMe online donation page so people could give money to help our family.

I shook my head. I hated the idea of taking other people's hard-earned money. But Dad saw it differently.

"People love your family. They have a strong desire to help. They want to be involved," he said encouragingly. "This is another way people can show their support. Why rob them of a blessing in helping you?"

I mulled over his words. I remembered all the times I had helped others, not only because I wanted to but also because I was called by God to do it. Natalie and I discussed it at length with my parents, and in the end, we agreed to do it.

In the weeks to come, hundreds of people donated. It was a huge blessing not having to stress about paying our bills, especially when we had so many other things to worry about.

When I thought about all the people who helped me, I had a huge sense of appreciation. Natalie and I both had been so committed to serving and helping others that it was awkward to be on the receiving end. Since my accident, we had relied on the body of Christ.

I knew how much the small stuff mattered because I saw it when I almost died.

Intercessory prayers from those who petitioned God to heal me. Acts of encouragement like visits, phone calls, and notes. Acts of service like people taking on extra work because I was unable to do my job. Practical gifts like delicious home-cooked meals people made for us. And sacrificial gifts like cash donations that paid our expenses associated with the accident.

I sat in my recliner and pondered the gratitude I felt. I thought of my near-death experience and remembered the movie screen with thousands of little moments. These actions of others were just like those little moments of my life that God allowed me to see. I knew beyond a shadow of a doubt how much the small stuff mattered because I saw it when I almost died.

Because God is holy, sin is sin. The indiscretions that seem small by human standards are equal to major transgressions in the way they separate us from God because all sin separates us from God. What if it was the same with goodness? Could token kindnesses be considered the same as extravagant, sacrificial acts before the Almighty? What if delivering an inspirational sermon that brought multitudes to Christ was the same as delivering a meal to a desperate family? Could earnestly interceding for someone in prayer be as pleasing to God as building an orphanage in a third-world country? What if it was all the same in God's economy? Goodness is goodness.

I've petitioned the Lord many times about the meaning for my life since I saw it flash before my eyes on that Saturday morning in October 2016. For me, it was a quick blur of everything I'd experienced. I was shown several snapshots, if you will, of Natalie, Cara, and Corban. I think God wanted me to see that love and people were most important of all. I think God wanted me to return to my body and do my best to cherish and fully love others.

God knew what I needed. He knew what would bring me the most joy, peace, hope, and encouragement. He also knew my struggle between my ministry and my family. I think God showed me Natalie, Cara, and Corbin—the people who are most important in my life—to remind me that they are my ministry too. I have no doubt that my purpose, my devotion, my calling, my ministry is to my family.

As I recuperated, people pondered spiritual questions: "Why would God let something this bad happen to someone on His team?" I'm a minister, and sometimes people think I have a special "in" with God. How could God allow me to be in such a horrific accident?

Some people were more accusatory. "Why did God do this to you?" they'd ask.

Sometimes people blame my accident on the evil one. They assume my fall was caused by Satan, who was messing up my life so I couldn't serve God anymore.

But for me, none of those scenarios fit. I believe in free will. My accident was just that—an accident. It happened. Neither God nor Satan caused it. It happened because I lost my balance and fell through glass. Period.

I do believe God allowed it to happen to me. Sure, He allowed me to fall, but He didn't cause me to fall. It just happened. But this I am sure of: God can use me and this accident for His glory.

I am sure of this: God can use me and this accident for His glory.

A favorite Scripture, one that most believers learn in their youth, is Romans 8:28 (KJV): "And we know that all things work together for good to them that love God, to them who are the called according to his purpose." That verse gives me strength. When I get down, I talk to God. I tell Him: "You know what, God? If You can make anything in this world turn out good, then You can bring good out of this situation."

Seeing Joy in Every Moment

About six months after the injury, I went back to work with modified duties. Every day I live in pain as a result of that freak accident in 2016. I've had years of occupational therapy and multiple surgeries to correct nerve damage, and I still have limited use of my left hand. Despite an ongoing struggle with regional pain, I'm getting better. I estimate that I've regained 60 percent of the strength and function of my left hand. Doctors say that in itself is a miracle. But the nerves still don't work quite right. I've tried all sorts of remedies for the pain—I even had signal blocks implanted in my spine. Nothing seems to help. But I'm holding on to the words in James 1:2–3 (NIV), the verse I learned at Hume Camp all those years ago. It's become my life verse: "Consider it pure joy, my brothers and sisters, whenever you face trials of many kinds, because you know that the testing of your faith produces perseverance."

As odd as it sounds, I count my traumatic experience as joy. I know I experienced a miracle. Being alive is a miracle. Being able to hold my wife and children is a miracle. God graciously gave us another miracle, a daughter, Camilla, born in 2018.

By saving my life, God has renewed my faith in Him and allowed me to see Him in a new way. And now He has allowed me to share this hope and joy of life with others because of my near-death experience and that movie screen—the realization that nothing is insignificant in God's kingdom. Every moment of life matters. Me. My service. My job. And yes, even my accident. No matter how seemingly routine or trivial an action, it all matters and has value.

My injuries have opened the door to share with others. I can tell them with deep assurance that no matter what is happening or how they feel, God sees. And it all counts. Even the most mundane moments of life are important to God. Nothing is insignificant.

My Life since My Near-Death Experience

Andrew Garcia

It's been more than four years since my NDE; I live with pain every day due to my accident, but I also feel a greater sense of love and peace because of my NDE.

Q Who was the first person you shared your experience with?

A I told Natalie about my near-death experience, but not until I left the hospital. I had been home for a couple of weeks. I was in a pretty fragile state at that time and talking about the experience was very emotional. She listened in a caring way and didn't say much.

Q Did your near-death experience change your relationship with God?

A Yeah, it did. I'm more focused on the things that He has called me to live out. I want to pursue the opportunities He's given to me—to share Him and His love with those around me. Before my accident, I was in a stale place, stale in my relationship with God. My near-death experience reignited my passion in sharing Jesus with the world.

Q *How did it change your relationship with your family?*

A It changed how I engage with them when I'm spending time with them. I try to be present. I fail constantly, but I have a desire in my heart to be better.

Q *Has the intensity of your near-death experience lessened over the years?*

A Yes. I find myself being lazy. I have to remind myself constantly that I had this amazing experience. It changed me at the moment and shortly after I returned. When I realize I'm falling back into old patterns, I try to remind myself of the things I learned. I made a commitment to God to love my family and not take things for granted.

Q *During your near-death experience, did you see a glimpse of your future?*

A I did not, but since I've been back, I feel this overwhelming sense that God has something more for me. I don't know exactly what that purpose is, but I do know that part of it is to live a different life, to be more intentional, and to lead others to live differently.

I have clear recollection of seeing all those pictures like a movie screen. Although I don't know exactly what was on every little screen, I know they were about experiences with people in my life, in the relationships I had. Over the years, I have randomly reached out to friends, to stay connected and to see how they are doing. I put more value in my relationships.

Never Alone

By Alma Blasquez, as told to Ginger Rue

*There is nothing so moving—not even acts of love
or hate—as the discovery that one is not alone.*

Robert Ardrey

When I felt the seizure coming on, I knew it would be severe. I could feel it in my spine. I'd had so many seizures in the months after the car accident that I'd gained an expertise at predicting the intensity of each one. Even though I had an extremely high fever, I was able to follow my usual pre-seizure routine: I centered myself as best I could in the hospital bed, wrapping first my ankles, then my wrists, with the bedsheet so I wouldn't flail. I tried to brace myself mentally as well, but I could never have prepared myself for what I was about to experience.

An Incredible Journey

Some have described it as a tunnel, but the place I was in was endless, without walls, shapeless. I was suspended in this peaceful, silvery void.

I was in this void for only two to three seconds before I came out of it into another realm. I first saw the most beautiful blue sky; then

I looked down at my feet. The ground under them was made of diamonds—not cut and faceted, but smooth and crystal clear. I was told to look down by a strong male voice that was both audible and transmitted through thoughts. In a small sliver of the diamond ground, I could see the entire round earth far below. It was almost like seeing the land from an airplane. I could see the outline of the entire planet.

I said to myself, I just died.

It wasn't like being in outer space; I didn't see any galaxies or asteroids or anything of that nature, but I could see that the earth had a light around it, like an aura. But it wasn't the same earth I'd ever seen on a map. This earth was brand new. The continents were all put together, like on the maps of Pangaea that show the land as one entire piece before continental drift occurred. I could see the green of trees and plants in the healthiest, freshest hue. The rest of the planet was water, its shade the most vivid, true blue—not turquoise or powder blue or any other shade—just untinted, pure blue. I said to myself, *I just died.*

During this time, I was never in silence, but the sound I heard is difficult to describe. Imagine if you heard a hundred symphonies playing at once, all ending their final note at the same moment. Think of the resonance lingering in the air from those last notes played simultaneously by every single instrument. Now think of the sound of a light bulb when it's switched on. What would you call that humming sound it makes? You might say it's the sound of the energy flowing through the light bulb. And that was what I heard—an energy. I think of it as the energy of angels flowing through the universe.

I looked back up to see mounds of huge, faceted diamonds scattered along the ground, all growing taller and taller in the distance. Each and every diamond was perfect in cut, clarity, and color, and each reflected a beautiful light, causing the entire terrain to sparkle. But where was the light coming from?

I looked all around and saw what I thought were souls of the dead. Each soul emitted light. I could not see my own body; I could only feel it. And though I could not see myself, I could see light coming from me—the same light that was coming from the other souls. My aura was glistening! The light that the diamonds reflected came not only from these shining, illumined souls, but also from me. A feeling of great joy washed over me.

The gate of heaven was not far. It was right down the path in front of me. The path looked like it was a chiseled mixture of gold, copper, and bronze. At the end of it, I could see a large stone gate. I wouldn't call it marble; the stone I saw was far more precious. It was breathtaking. I knew immediately that this was the gate into heaven, morphing into eternity, having no end. Through the gate, I saw levels, like a cascading, upward flow of stairs or realms.

Between the gate and me was a giant orb of white light—whiter than any white we could fathom here on earth. And although the orb was immense, and its white light more intense than any light I'd ever witnessed, I understood that this light was not God.

For all its beauty, for all its power beyond my human comprehension, this light was merely a shadow of the fullness of the Almighty.

The light was almost too much to take in, and I believe it shielded me from seeing His complete glory. Therefore, because I cannot call this orb of light "God in All His Fullness," I have come to call it the "Great Glisten of the Eye of God."

The joy that had washed over me only moments before was suddenly replaced by some trepidation: judgment. I knew that I had not been perfect in life, of course, but I hoped that I had died bravely and that this would improve my case.

I asked the Glisten, "Didn't I die with courage?" Thin, fiber-like wisps of light came forth from the orb and touched my body where I had been injured physically in the car accident. It also somehow seemed to heal me from the emotional injuries I suffered during my lifetime. I was awestruck. How could I, a mortal, an imperfect human being, stand in even this partial presence of God?

I pondered the question in my heart. I had been taught from a young age that I was filled with sin. I feared for a moment, again, this thing called judgment. Yet somehow, I became courageous and ready to be judged to enter the gate before me, even though being in this light revealed my earthly guilt and shame. I had been sexually abused as a child, and it had caused me to feel worthless. Those feelings of shame had led me to distrust people and had made it difficult for me to feel love from others.

Prior to the accident, I was able to stay busy, distracting myself from the memories of abuse. But after being struck by a car in adulthood, I had time to dwell on the past, and it became difficult for me to forgive others as Jesus had taught.

I began to tell the light how unworthy I was, how sinful I had been at times. But each time I had a negative thought about myself, a wisp of light came from the orb and touched me and took the negative thoughts away. I began to stand straighter and straighter, feeling my body and standing correctly for the first time in years. I could feel myself being healed by those wisps of light, in body, mind, and spirit.

I became lost in the beauty of the diamond ground and gate of heaven morphing into forever, entranced by the peace. I heard the same strong voice I'd heard before. This time it came from my left and called to me in words I heard audibly.

I was given a life review and that showed me I was "good" and full of worth to Him.

I moved to see where this voice was coming from and saw it was the orb I call the Glisten, swirling toward me and saying, "You are here because you have come to me often." Then it stopped right in front of me where I was standing.

The Glisten told me things about myself as it healed me. I was given a life review that showed me I was "good" and full of worth to Him. The last thing it said was that the next time I heard its audible voice, it would tell me something I had to do upon my return to live again.

Then the light began to recede. Without words, I called out to it. *No! What happened? I was going into heaven! What is happening?* But the light moved farther and farther away until it receded and I saw only the ceiling of the hospital room. The light was gone.

In the moment that followed my separation from the light, my heart held two opposing forces at once: profound grief and profound joy. I could not bear the thought of leaving the presence of the light. And yet I was also overcome by joy, grateful for the love and acceptance that God had poured into me only moments before.

Although I'd desperately wanted to stay, it was not meant for me to enter the gate of heaven at that moment. I prayed that someday, by God's grace, I would return.

When I found myself back in my hospital bed and in my body, I had a feeling of being constricted, as though my body were too small a space to hold my spirit. I became more aware of my breathing with each passing moment as if I were brand-new.

It took me years to process my moment at the gate of heaven.

The next sound I heard was a gasp.

"I thought you were dead," said my hospital roommate, her voice trembling with fear. "You had another one of them seizures. I was going to let the nurse find you in the morning. I don't touch dead people."

Her eyes were wide, as though she'd just seen a ghost, as they say. And that's when it hit me that I could see her face—that I had turned my head to look at her. For the first time in nine years, I had been able to move the three severely degenerating upper cervical discs in my neck.

Many Encounters

That part of the story is only a portion of all that I experienced on that particular day at about four o'clock in the morning in March of 2012, when I was fifty-four years old. And it's only a portion of the heavenly encounters I have experienced over the course of my life. Just being able to tell even that abbreviated version of my story has been a long and arduous journey. It took me years to process my moment at the gate of heaven, even though I could speak of my experience right away with a few of my closest supportive friends.

Dealing with the conflicting overwhelming emotions was one challenge, but beyond the emotional challenges were the intellectual ones. The experience left me with so many questions, the greatest of which was simply this: *Why didn't I stay?*

Our souls yearn to be in the presence of God, and I had personally stood in the presence of the Great Glisten of His Eye. In that fleeting moment, I was so much closer to Him than I could be here on this earth and in this body.

And yet, that day in 2012 was not the first time I had been in the presence of God. When I was a small child in the early 1960s, under the age of five, I encountered God on three separate occasions when I was held by the Holy Spirit. The first time, I was two and a half years old. The other times, I was three and a half, then four and a half. I also had a clear vision of Jesus when I was five and a half.

Childhood Trauma

I was born in Chicago, but when I was a month old, my father started a large business in Mexico, and we moved there. I arrived severely dehydrated from a failure to nurse properly. Only a blood transfusion from my father saved my young life. We stayed in Mexico for two years before returning to Chicago. At that time, our core family consisted of my parents, my two older brothers, me, and my maternal grandmother, who lived with our family until I was nearly thirty years old. I trusted my grandmother completely and was more bonded to her than anyone else in the world. She was many things to me, including my protector.

From the outside, our family looked picture perfect. Thanks to my father's job as a draftsman, we were one of the more prosperous families in our neighborhood. We had a nice home with beautiful furniture. My parents had many friends and frequently entertained.

My ex-air-force-pilot father was extremely handsome and looked like the movie star Tony Curtis; my gorgeous mother resembled a young Elizabeth Taylor. In old photographs, we seemed to embody the American dream. But when I look at my young face in these pictures, I see a child filled with extreme sadness. I remember that child well: the mute little girl. I had stopped talking at around age three and did not speak more than a few syllables for almost a full year.

God did not leave me forsaken during my horrible ordeals.

I understand now that "elective mutism" is an anxiety disorder common in children who are abused, a response to trauma. Beginning when I was two and a half and continuing for many years, I was abused. By the time I was twelve years old, I felt more like a hundred.

God did not leave me forsaken during these horrible ordeals, however. He gave me my grandmother, who loved me fiercely and served as my earthly protector as best she could, and He held me during my darkest times. When I say God held me, I do not mean metaphorically. I mean that God literally held me. In my childhood, I had learned about Jesus and the Holy Spirit, and so I knew who was holding me.

On one occasion, I recall being cradled, as if I were in a huge, warm blanket or a soft down comforter. I could sense a large presence—a gentle giant, perhaps—holding me, filling me with light. I was fully bathed in this full, bright white light. I felt perfect peace. That was my first experience of going to another place, of not being on this earth. I was gone for what seemed like a long time. I can't say how long it lasted, but I know it was significant. I had a sense of eternal peace and felt completely loved. And completely safe.

I saw an immense white light looking down at me and could see the same amount of light coming up from this giant's arm. Light was all around me. I could feel this giant, this Comforter, looking at me as He held me. I now understand that I was being held by the Holy Spirit. I had always compared the feeling of being held to being wrapped in a comforter, but in fact, the word *Comforter* is what Jesus uses in John 14:16 when he says, "And I will pray the Father, and he shall give you another Comforter, that he may abide with you for ever." (KJV) I could feel that sense of being held and never alone in the truest sense.

Another experience with the Comforter was very much the same. Although I went up into the light again, where I was cradled and loved, this time, the Comforter spoke to me. "I am with you," He said. "You are with Me. You are safe in My love." I inhaled the strong aroma of what I can only describe as being similar to a thousand of the most beautiful roses that had ever or would ever exist on earth.

When I was almost five, my grandmother learned what had been happening. From then on and as long as she lived, my grandmother stayed by my side as best she could. When she could not be with me, God sent me angels.

Entertaining Angels

I was about five when I met one of my two guardian angels for the first time. This angel was large, but not as large as the Comforter. I can't call the angel "he" or "she" because it was more of a light than a person. It had human features but was made up of a bright light that at times appeared opaque. The angel was maybe a foot taller than I was at that age. It felt to me like an older sibling. It was very beautiful, engaging, and joyful. I think God sent it to me because I had stopped talking to people, but I would talk with this angel. It played with me.

All day, every day, it stayed always on my right side. The other angel was my protector angel, whom I would meet a short time later.

> *I had stopped talking to people, but I would talk with my angel.*

When I started school, my first angel who played with me would tell me when to help others. I was enrolled in the first grade at a Catholic school. My parents thought my silence was a sign of maturity and obedience. The angel helped me make friends at school because I could see the angels with other children. I could see their angels, and they could see mine. Eventually, I began talking with the other children whose angels I could see. My schoolmates and I delighted in speaking to one another about our angels.

Every Friday at Catholic school, we had Stations of the Cross, which is a series of depictions of Jesus on the day of His crucifixion. Each depiction represents one of fourteen points on Jesus's path to Calvary, and we would stop at each station to meditate on those moments and pray. My friends who had angels and I would look at one another at each station, and we would become very emotional. We understood the sovereignty of Jesus and felt sadness for what He had endured.

I remember that my angel would say to me, "Do not cry. It's not time to cry," and I would not cry. My friends would look at me and follow my lead. When we got to the second-to-last station, my angel would say, "It's almost time for you to cry." Then, of course, when we would get to the station where Jesus is on the cross and lastly when His mother is holding Him, my angel would say, "You can cry now." Then my friends, as if waiting for my cue from my angel, would cry also.

The nuns did not like this. They told my parents that I was too young to be in that school, so my parents put me in public kindergarten. I was heartbroken. At public school I started to have some difficulties. School officials thought I was autistic because I did not talk, but at that time, autism was not widely known about or understood, so they didn't really know what to make of me.

No one pieced together that I had been an abuse victim. Instead, they sat me in a room by myself and gave me many puzzle-type tests for many weeks. When my scores showed that I was highly intelligent, the school officials stopped worrying about me and returned me to a classroom.

In the secular environment of public school, I could not understand many of my classmates. I could not see their angels. I asked some children if they had angels, and some said yes, and others said no. It upset me to learn that not everyone could see angels. That was when my protector angel showed up. My guardian angel remained to my right, and my protector angel stayed to my left but always walked a full step in front of me. I knew that this angel was there to protect and comfort me. When I was picked on by anyone, I would call on my angels to be with me, and they would immediately be there.

The few other children who saw angels became my friends, and whenever they would run up to link arms with me, my angels would make room for them. It was a beautiful time. We would all giggle and laugh and walk to the playground together before the school day began. My angels told me that if I would talk to other children, I would make more friends, so I began talking again. I found that I had a special gift for empathy. When a friend had an issue or a problem, I could sense it and would ask if I could help. My angels would tell me what I should say.

A Vision of Jesus

I began to feel safe again. I was about five and a half. I remember playing outside one sunny Saturday afternoon. It must have been high noon, because I clearly recall seeing the sun straight up above me. I was leaning on my father's Cadillac, the kind that had tail fins that looked to me like wings. I was pretending that my father was driving and that the wind was blowing through my hair as our whole family drove cross-country.

When I heard the voices, I knew they were saints having a conversation.

Anyone looking on would have said I was playing alone, but I knew my angels were with me. We were all having incredible enjoyment during this summer of freedom, as I felt it to be.

I looked up into the sky and saw beautiful clouds. Then I heard voices. When I'd gone to Catholic school as a small child, they had taught us that saints and angels were in heaven and that they would gather to talk about us and work in our lives. So when I heard the voices, I knew they were the saints just having a conversation. I could hear individual words for about a minute. I heard one of them say, "Look at God's beautiful children that we take care of."

Then there were many voices—so many at once that I couldn't make out one word from another. Then Jesus walked out of a cloud. As He came down toward me, I remember squinting my eyes and thinking, *Is this really happening?* I closed my eyes completely for a second, then opened them again. He was closer. I closed them once more, and when I opened my eyes, He was standing right in front of me.

His left hand was on His heart, and His right hand was in the air, with two fingers up but sort of cupped, curved. Giant rays of golden light surrounded Him, and this light also radiated from His heart straight to my heart and body. I could see Him clearly. He was dressed in a beige, ruby-red, and purple cloak. He was the size of a regular human man, not giant like the Comforter. He looked like a young man. I remember feeling somewhat frightened, but with His eyes, He told me not to be afraid.

Then He said, "I am with you, I have always been with you, and I will always be with you." I stared at His beauty for a full moment, not knowing what to say or do.

I panicked at hearing the future tense "will be." I knew why He had been with me in the past. I felt that Jesus was warning me that He would be with me when more bad things happened to me in the future. I was terrified of what was to come.

Walking Away

I tried to remember Jesus's promise that He would be with me through the painful times. The abuse stopped before I reached my teen years, but by then, I was so filled with feelings of worthlessness that I began to question God, as if He had gone from my life. I thought of

Allowing myself to experience the angelic presence gave me a special understanding of life.

running away or committing suicide. I wanted to just disappear. I begged God and my angels to take me out of this world. I sank into a depression so deep it was a force all its own, determined to fully take me over. Eventually, I stopped speaking to my angels. I thought they had left because I was bad and I didn't deserve them.

Thinking I was unworthy of having angels or the love of Christ, I turned into a quiet, disrespectful teenager, thankfully for only about two years. I had learned in church that we were supposed to be perfect, like Jesus, and that we were born into sin. Our culture had taught me that I was filled with sin. I started to think this was why all the terrible things in my life had happened to me, and I believed I deserved it all.

Life-Changing Accident

It was never God's will for His light to be dimmed in my life; I dimmed it at my own choosing. As I grew into a young woman and started college, I eventually stopped blocking God's influence in my life. I embraced God's presence and could feel my angels with me once more.

In early adulthood, I saw my angels differently. They were no longer distinct presences, but more like balls of light, like small stars I could actually see. Allowing myself to experience the angelic presences again gave me a special understanding of life. When I could see the bright light and feel my angels with me, things were good. But the angels would also warn me about bad things to come by giving me visions of the future. I would have waking dreams of dark events to come. Through them, I predicted the murder of a family friend, another friend's illness, and the death of my own father.

Once, after my daughter was born, I had a vision of her having a grand mal seizure at five years old. When she was away visiting her grandparents that year, I got the call that my daughter had had a seizure, but I already knew. No one could understand how I knew. Whenever I shared my visions with my family, they brushed them off, but I had loving friends who believed me and were my gifts from God.

I suppose one might say I was successful in life. I did well in school, earning my undergraduate, masters, and doctoral degrees, all with the highest honors. I bought a nice home with my own money. I had a good marriage for some time. I had many interesting careers, including working as a police officer and crime analyst before teaching special-needs children, many who were nonverbal and from abusive homes. I related to these children in a special way. I guess it took me back full circle to when I was a nonverbal child myself.

But my adult life was far from easy. In September 2003, when I was in my early forties, I was involved in a car accident. By this time I was recently divorced with an eleven-year-old daughter, who was a beautiful gift from God. I felt so incredibly blessed to be her mother. Doctors had told me I'd never be able to have children, so she had come as a giant surprise from the Lord. Even though my marriage to her father had not succeeded, my daughter and I were happy.

Before I knew it, the hood of the taxi had hit me, and I went flying through the air.

We lived in Chicago, and one balmy Saturday afternoon, I decided to ride my bike to the annual parents' potluck at my daughter's school. My mother was babysitting my daughter, and the school was only a short distance from my house.

I had discovered years ago that being physically active helped my mind stay away from the negative messages I had believed about myself as a child. I'd been on the cross-country running team when I'd first started college, and I'd continued to stay in great shape when I went through the police academy. I was an amateur bodybuilder, runner, bicyclist, and swimmer. I was also the top-ranking player on my local tennis and soccer teams. I felt in control of my life and relished my roles as a mother, a teacher, and an athlete.

I rode my bicycle almost everywhere, so it wasn't a big deal for me to ride to my daughter's school that day. When the traffic light signaled the cars to stop at an intersection, I looked both ways before crossing. Suddenly a taxi made a U-turn. I screamed, "No!"

Before I knew it, the hood of the taxi had hit me, and I went flying through the air, then began falling face down. I curled my head down into the handlebars to break the fall so I wouldn't land on my face. The last thing I remember before losing consciousness was landing on the handlebars with my torso. When I woke up lying in the street, I was surrounded by people. Some were touching me and trying to help me stay put; they'd already taken the bike away.

The first words out of my mouth were, "I have to go get him [the taxi driver]. I have to get on my bike!" Someone in the crowd said, "Stay down! Help is on the way." I began to pray.

The paramedics arrived, along with the fire department. By this time, I was trying to move, trying to get up and see what was hurt, whether any bones were broken. I found I couldn't move much at all. The paramedics put me on a stretcher and took me to the emergency room. I gave them my mother's number so that someone could call her and my daughter and let them know about the accident.

As I lay on the examination table in the X-ray lab, I overheard some of the nurses saying, "She doesn't have insurance." I wondered who they were talking about. It couldn't have been me. As a teacher in the Chicago public school system for the past six years, I had a great medical plan. Although I had excelled as a teacher, I was transferred to a different school system just before the academic year began. I had called out an administrator after I learned that he had molested one of my students, and I believe he transferred me to get rid of me. I had no idea, until then, that he had secretly made me a "ghost payrollee," effectively canceling my insurance.

A man came into the room and began taking me off the X-ray table rather forcefully. "You can't be here," he said. "You have to go." He named another hospital where I would be sent. He said it was because I had no insurance.

I refused to go to the other hospital the man had named. I knew its reputation as a substandard place for the uninsured. I called my ex-husband, who picked me up from the hospital and took me to my mother's house.

The Aftermath

For the next week, I rested and prayed. I was able to walk after a few days, but I had a limp. I also had a dislocated jaw and severe internal injuries because the handlebars had pushed my organs into a sort of giant mass to the right side of my torso cavity. My digestive system was thrown into complete turmoil. I had to begin liquefying my diet because of the difficulty in processing solid food. I lost a lot of weight. I would need several reconstructive surgeries if I hoped to have any sort of a normal life again.

I was becoming more and more depressed as my health declined.

Still, I went back to work. I couldn't lose my job at my new school. My checks still showed payroll deductions for health coverage, so no one in the system could explain why I didn't have insurance. I wound up having to sue the principal in order to get the surgeries my doctors said I would need after the accident. Eight months after I filed suit, my insurance was reinstated, but it was too late to get the jaw surgery I needed, and I needed to postpone my back surgeries until the summer. I'd already had three surgeries to reconstruct both my upper and lower intestines and my bladder.

By this point, I could barely move. I had to sit in a chair in the front of the classroom and teach while sitting down. When I explained to the children that I'd been in an accident and this was the reason I didn't stand up to teach, they were very sweet and understanding. They helped me as much as they could. But one day, after I had picked them up from the lunchroom and was standing in the hallway with them, I just collapsed. Right in the middle of speaking to my students, I lost all strength and fell on the floor. I couldn't move.

From that day forward, I could barely stand at all. I had to give up driving. I had to start taking the bus, but oftentimes, the driver had to help me on and off. It was difficult to realize how crippled I'd become. I had been so physically active before the accident and was suddenly becoming barely able to move. It was devastating.

I desperately needed to keep my job, but my new principal was not happy with me. Not only was I absent much of the time, but she was also wary of me because she knew I had sued my last principal over the insurance issue. More than a year after the accident, I was in so much pain that I could no longer postpone the surgeries I needed, and I had to take medical leave. The surgeries were long and arduous, and afterward, I was in a coma for about six to seven hours.

After I finally recovered from the surgeries, I was diagnosed with lupus, degenerative spine disease, and a muscle atrophy disease that meant my muscles were sinking into my bone. Of course, I was becoming more and more depressed as my health declined, so in addition to the pain pills, the doctors prescribed antidepressants and antianxiety medications. I only sank into a deeper depression. As it had in my teen years, the depression seemed to be a living foe, working its way into my body and mind and eventually into my spirit, convincing me I had no control over my life.

To make the depression worse, my old childhood nightmares of monsters who looked like men returned. I couldn't rest well, and my health deteriorated even further. By 2010 I had nine degenerated discs in my back. Three spine specialists said I needed additional surgery and that if I didn't have it, I would die an excruciatingly painful death. I was in so much pain, but I did not want to have the spinal surgeries. I also stopped taking the antidepressant and antianxiety medications. They were not helping and were only clouding my mind. I told God, "If I'm going to die, I want to die with a clear mind to see You in full."

Hoping for Death

I'd suffered for six long years after the main abdominal surgeries and thought death would be easier than living this way. To allow this mortal body to pass was not an issue for me. My only concerns were of leaving my daughter, who was a junior in college and living with me at the time, and of meeting God. I was terrified at the thought of being judged by God. I still carried so much shame from my child-

A bright light appeared to me. My protector angel had returned!

hood trauma. I had decided, at some point after the accident, that my illness must have been a punishment due to my sin. I thought that I must have been born with so much original sin that I had deserved to be hit by that taxi, that I deserved the resulting complications from it, and that I deserved to have a short life.

Some dear friends, a married couple, took me in around the Christmas holidays in 2011. They said, "We will not allow you to be in this condition by yourself," and they insisted I come stay with them. God bless these friends! One day while I was there, I got out of bed and felt something hurting in one particular area of my back. It felt like a cold wind was going through me in one spot. I touched the spot and felt a hole. My skin had separated there and a sort of ulcer had formed—a bedsore. By the start of January 2012, that bedsore developed into full-body shingles.

On top of everything else, shingles was devastatingly painful. My life was more than I could bear.

I begged God to let me die of a major heart attack: "I would be most grateful. I don't want to suffer anymore. I don't want to linger. I don't want my daughter to see me like this. Please just take me quickly."

I had over a dozen prescriptions I was taking at that point. To speed the process of death along, I began weaning myself off all of them. This caused me to have major seizures. During one of the seizures, I flailed so much that I began to fall out of bed. A bright light appeared to me. My protector angel had returned! The angel came to my side and held me until the seizure was over. I did not fall out of bed when I surely should have as I was one quarter off the bed and going down when my angel lifted me with its strength and put me back in bed.

Not only did I feel better physically for a few months, but all my thoughts of not being good enough also disappeared in the angel's light.

Eventually, the pain returned. By March of the following year, 2012, I was surprised and disappointed that I was still alive. I finally had to call a friend to take me to the emergency room, where I stayed for nearly ten hours, having multiple seizures before finally being admitted. In my hospital room, I was hooked up to an EKG machine and a feeding tube. I already looked like death: emaciated and hunched over, a shell of a person. For almost six years, I had not even been able to use the bathroom normally; it was agony.

One of the intern doctors asked me if I felt like dying, and I answered yes. What I meant was that I was tired of living this way, but they recorded it as a suicidal ideation, so I was transferred to the psychiatric ward.

I could acutely feel my special way of seeing people—not just their bodies but also their auras.

The psych ward was a terrifying place. I saw the staff holding people down, forcing them to be injected with drugs. Other patients were walking around like zombies. But I could see more than just their physical bodies. The empathy and visions I had begun having as a child had stayed with me to varying degrees throughout my adult life, and now I could acutely feel my special way of seeing people. I saw not just their bodies but also their auras. I could see that these were innocent people. Somewhere along the way in their lives, they'd been given the same message I had been given as a child: that they were not worth loving. I felt a kinship with them.

When I was admitted, I heard the staff talking about me. "She's so thin," one nurse said. "And look at the way her veins are sticking out." She turned to me. "How often do you use these veins?"

I didn't understand the question. Didn't we all use our veins all the time? "Every day," I replied.

"You keep them very clean," she said. "No marks." Marks? What did she mean? I thought immediately about the marks in Jesus's hands and suddenly lost myself in longing for Him.

Meanwhile, the nurse turned back to her colleague. "Heroin addict," she concluded.

Is This Heaven?

As I lay in bed in the psychiatric unit, emaciated and broken in body, I was glad, in a way, when the seizures started again. I hoped they meant impending death, and I longed to be free of my suffering. When I could feel in my entire spine that the oncoming seizure would be severe, I hoped it would be the last.

I wanted to cross over from this life, but I don't know exactly what I expected. When I found myself in the silvery atmosphere of the void, and then standing on diamond ground that stretched into forever, I remember saying to myself, "Oh my. I've just died."

When I looked up from seeing the earth beneath me under the clear spot in the diamond path, I looked up to see the most beautiful blue sky. To my far left was a waterfall. In front of me, the huge gate of heaven. Beyond the gate was a wall, preventing me from seeing inside entirely. There was also a wall to my right, leading up to the gate. I wanted to know how far the wall went, and the answer seemed to be that it went on forever. I wanted to walk toward heaven's gate, but I was not moving.

I looked down and saw that the diamond ground under the path to the gate of heaven became like beautiful sand made of tiny diamonds. I remember thinking, *I'm really here. Prayer is real. I have to let my daughter, Mercedes, know.* When I thought of my daughter, I saw a spark of light come out of my heart. Then I thought, *Everyone should know.* I thought of all the beauty I had experienced on earth, every lovely scent I'd ever smelled, every beautiful animal, flower, and tree I had ever seen, every person in my life. It occurred to me that I would never experience those things again, and I thought of how I would miss them.

And yet, nothing on earth could compare with the sensory overload of beauty in this place...the sights, the sound of angelic energy, the beautiful aroma.

Suddenly an angel picked me up from the diamond ground and took me to the waterfall.

That was when I heard the voice I heard so long ago: *You are here because you've come to me often. Continue to do what you have been doing.* I thought that meant to continue the process of leaving my earthly life to enter heaven, so I prepared myself to continue to listen well and stand astutely while taking in this knowledge from the Great Glisten. I had done ROTC in high school, so I knew how to stand straight like a soldier. I tried my best to stand tall as I tried to walk. I wanted to walk toward the gate. I could still feel the pain in my back, and I knew I had a fever.

Trying to take it all in was overwhelming. Thousands of other souls were standing to my right, to my left, and behind me. I looked at one person in particular on my right. It was a man. I could see every outline of his being but could not say what he looked like or who he was. I somehow thought that the souls surrounding me were others who had passed away at the same time I had.

I said something to the Great Glisten about how I was ready to be judged. I felt that I was taking up too much of His time and that He had all these other souls to take care of. Such an earthly thought to have in the heavenly realm, but I was concerned about "holding up the line." I suppose I had some inkling of the connection all souls have, because I felt compassion for them. I wanted to make room for them so they would have time with the Great Glisten as well. I could hear voices behind the gate, and I desperately wanted to go in, but I was not yet permitted.

I asked, "How is it that I am talking with You? I know I died. I don't feel like I'm breathing. How can I talk when I'm not breathing?"

The Glisten answered, "Because I breathe for you. I have always been breathing for you." I felt so satisfied with this answer and so intensely loved that I just wanted to go with the Glisten wherever it would take me.

Suddenly an angel (I felt one) picked me up from the diamond ground and took me to the waterfall I'd seen to my left. As I approached it, I could see it wasn't really made of water. It was thicker, somewhere between the consistency of water and gel. The water had all the colors of the rainbow in it, and it shimmered like liquid diamonds.

My angels laid me on the most amazing grass nearby. I could see each individual blade of grass move toward the light. Each blade was so alive and seemed to welcome me. As I lay on the grass, I felt my fever leave me in an instant. The grass, each blade its own life, was loving me and healing me. The pinky finger of my left hand barely touched the diamond gel-water, and when this happened, I felt my fever disappear entirely. Then the angels picked me back up and brought me to the spot where I had been standing moments before.

Next, the Glisten asked me to turn to my right. When I did, I saw my maternal grandmother, my protector, and three of her sisters and a man. On my left, I saw my paternal grandmother and three other relatives from that side of my family. My father was there, too, but only for a split second. He stepped out from the right and moved to my left. I didn't see him move to the left, but I saw him on that side. He smiled at me, and then he disappeared. I didn't see him again. At the time, I did not understand what this meant, but years later, I understood. When he was alive, my father used to say that when he died, he was going to ask God to let him travel the galaxies for all eternity to take in the beauty. I think he was granted that request and stopped just to see me for a moment before he continued his journey.

When I looked back at my grandmother, my earthly protector I adored, she was smiling. I said hello to her with my eyes. She seemed happy to see me, which was what I thought was supposed to happen in heaven—that we are supposed to be greeted by lost loved ones in a joyous reunion. But I noticed that no one else among those thousands of souls seemed happy.

Something instructed me to look specifically at these souls. There were more rows than I could count. On the first row, the one I could see the most clearly, the souls were completely humanlike: I could see the outline of the human figure, with the head, neck, ears, shoulders, elbows, hands, hips, knees—everything in outline.

The souls were all different sizes, just like humans on earth. Some were heavyset, some were thinner; others were taller; some were more muscular. And they all were a beautiful blue color. I was told, "Look closer." That was when I realized they were all made out of water. I looked more deeply and realized that together, they made up a vast body of water.

I said, "We are mostly water," and a voice said, "Yes." When one soul moved, all the others moved as well, and I could hear the movement like a great symphony. I began to understand that somehow, no matter how many souls or how far removed, we all touch other lives in some way, and they touch ours.

But why were they so somber? Did they know something I did not?

I had a moment of great concern. Maybe the others were not smiling because I was about to be judged. I would

When I looked at my grandmother, she was smiling.

have to own up to every single thing I ever thought or did. I might not be allowed into heaven at all. Perhaps this was what purgatory was like, waiting to be allowed into heaven. Perhaps I would be standing here forever. I would have gladly swept the floors of heaven for all eternity just to be allowed in. But now that I was at the gate of heaven, I prepared to be judged.

I turned my eyes away from the wall and saw a gigantic orb of white, white light—the purest white. The orb had sped toward me, spinning its light around me. Then it stopped right in front of me. I thought, *This is a part of God.* I waited with courage for judgment that would come. How could I stand in even a partial presence of God? Although I knew I was unworthy, I hoped that the way I had welcomed death without fear might help my cause. I had come prepared to face the things I had done in my life, and I had no thought of trying to excuse them. I asked the orb, "Didn't I die with courage?"

In response, the orb, the Great Glisten of the Eye of God, gave off immense rays of light. Each ray was a wisp that was navy blue toward the end of it, and within that navy blue was an iridescent rainbow. On each end, about three or four inches from the tip, was a bead about an inch around that was solid pink and navy blue, illuminated with rainbow colors. The wisps of light touched me, and I could feel a healing light touching my spirit. I no longer feared judgment because the light purified me.

Nothing else mattered except being here, surrounded in this feeling of perfect love.

Although I had begun to confess all my sins, the wisps removed these thoughts. Every negative thought I had about myself disappeared, and as my spirit was healed, I began to stand straighter and taller. The whiteness of the wisp healed me, and the blue part of the bead took away the negative thoughts, while the pink part of it left me with the opposite of each negative thought. After each wisp touched me, it retracted into the orb.

In an instant, I stopped worrying about taking up too much time. I forgot about everything connected to earthly life, everything I had thought about moments before that I would miss, even my beloved daughter. Nothing else mattered except being here, surrounded in this feeling of perfect love.

As the light touched me, I felt that it was making me ready to enter the gate, cleansing me. I asked the Glisten, "Is this heaven?" and I was told that it was. I asked another question: "Is the wall of heaven...is that eternity? It looks like it goes on forever."

Immediately I was answered. "They're all mine," a voice said. "Yes, they are all mine." I couldn't understand the meaning. Why was the voice referring to eternity, a singular thing, as a plural? But I dared not ask for explanation. After all, who was I to question God? I just wanted to go in so badly. Still, I couldn't help but ask the question that had followed me my entire life: "Why did those things happen to me when I was a young child?"

Was It My Fault?

I suppose the real question that I couldn't bring myself to ask was, "Did I deserve it?" Abuse, especially from a family member and at such a young age, can lead the victim to such a place of shame that there's always a lingering question of culpability. Had I done something or was I born so evil that I somehow deserved what had happened to me?

The sand under my feet moved like a wave of water, then stopped suddenly and made a slight dip. The golden bronze-copper road that followed the sand also made a slight dip before the gate of heaven. I didn't know what this dip meant.

A second light came out of the right side of the Glisten of the Eye of God. This light was bright golden yellow, beautiful and vibrant. It glowed so brightly that the white light dimmed itself to allow this beautiful golden yellow light to dominate. I knew somehow that this golden yellow light was Jesus. Its rays came down to meet me at my feet just as it had when I was a little girl. I could not speak.

I could feel the purest love coming from this yellow light. I did not ask it anything. I was told, "Just accept." I had never been able to accept that I was worth loving, not even as I stood at the gate of heaven. But now, I did accept the love offered to me. When I finally understood that I had to accept this unconditional love, the bright golden yellow light went back into the giant white light, and they became one again.

A ledge that looked like it was made of marble came out of the orb and hovered in the air. On the ledge was large drawing paper like artists use. One of the wisps from the Glisten came out without a bead. It was just a plain, white wisp, and it caught the paper, creating a spark.

I knew those bursts of light were angels there with us.

"This is your conception," I was told. Then that sheet of paper was put off to the side, as if filed away. Another sheet of art paper appeared, showing me myself at one and a half years old. It was like watching a movie of myself. I was chasing a butterfly, and the butterfly was saying to me, "Come play with me! Play with me!" as I giggled and laughed. The Glisten wanted to show me that I had been a normal, playful little girl and that for a time, everything in my life had been well. This was my life review. Next, I was shown myself in a little pinafore dress in a park where my family used to have picnics.

The review jumped to me at seven years old on the school playground, helping a classmate. I remembered him: Leo, a sweet, timid boy. He was telling me that someone wanted to fight with him and he was afraid. I told him I would go with him to talk to this person. That scene was filed away, and then came another scene when I was ten or twelve, helping another classmate.

More scenes appeared of me helping others until the age of about twenty. Then a burst of light, a little stardust, appeared between my friends and me in each of the scenes. I knew those bursts of light were our angels there with us. I was shown the rest of my life and told that

I would have more prophecy but that I must be very discerning about sharing those prophecies.

After the life review was complete, the Glisten put something into my heart. I was told that I was perfect, that I was made perfect. I never felt so loved.

I looked again at my relatives. They had slight smiles on their faces now. I expected them to lead me down the path, through the gate. I could feel their energy. I asked if I could enter. I was shown the inside of the gate, where I saw three huge tables made out of light. Bending over the first table were souls I would call saints. Their voices sounded like the ones I had heard from heaven when I was five on the day I saw the vision of Jesus. The saints wore long, beautiful off-white gowns and light was coming from their faces, like an aura. They were talking to one another, and I realized they were angelic souls watching over individuals on earth.

At the second table, it was the same. The table was the same size and full of light. Other beautiful beings were bent over it, with their auras of light coming out of their faces and the light coming up from the table, and they were talking too.

The third table was behind the other two and was much larger. It was far enough away from me that I could not hear exactly what the saints were saying, but there were many of them surrounding that table. They were talking about the planet, and the conversation was extremely serious. I knew they were talking about certain countries but could not decipher which ones.

I wanted to walk past those tables into heaven. I lifted my right leg to begin walking. As soon as I felt it lift, everything went silver again. I was again in the void. I opened my eyes and saw that the Glisten of the Eye of God was still there, so I felt happy. But the light slowly began to retreat. Just before the light was gone, the voice audibly repeated, "Continue to do what you have been doing."

The next thing I knew, I was staring at the ceiling of my hospital room. A complete sense of grief overtook me. *No*! I said in my mind and heart. *I was there! I was supposed to stay!*

Back in the Hospital

Back in my hospital bed, I felt every single nerve ending and pore and cell in my body. I knew right away that I could move my neck without pain. I moved my midback to face my roommate a little bit more. I was able to move my lower back. I knew that I was healed in heaven by this Great Glisten of the Eye of God and by Jesus. For years, I'd been bent over in a U-shape to avoid the intense pain of standing up.

> *I was joyous that I had been healed but could not understand why I'd come back.*

A complete sense of joy layered itself over the sense of grief. Although I was joyous that I'd been healed, I could not understand why I'd come back. My roommate asked me what had happened. All I could manage to say was, "I'm tired; you talk." It was too much to put into words.

After I'd slept for a while following the near-death experience, I woke up no longer feeling depressed. I'd been hiding my medications because I'd worked so hard to wean myself off them before being admitted to the psychiatric ward, and I didn't want to go backward. The nurses thought I took them because I'd pretend to swallow, but when they weren't looking, I'd spit the pills into a tissue and flush them down the toilet.

When he saw the change in me after my healing in heaven, a male nurse told me, "I know you don't belong here. It's a mistake. It happens a lot." He was a godsend, that young man. He told me if I wanted to be released, I needed to get out of bed and attend workshops so that I could get points. Once I had enough points, I would be released. My mother was not allowed to come and see me, so I decided to help the other people in the hospital who did not have family by walking around with them. Though my spine had been healed and I was no longer depressed, my muscles were weak from years of disuse, but it was good to be able to walk.

The hospital staff took note of my improved state of mind, and just like the male nurse had told me, I started accumulating points toward release.

While I was in the hospital, I told only one person a portion of my near-death experience, just a very abbreviated version. He was a dynamic and muscular guard—everyone was afraid of him. But I had the gift of seeing auras, and to me, he felt like an angel, so I knew I could trust him. I told him that I had gone somewhere not of this world and that I had met a giant orb of light. He believed me and promised to protect me from the medical staff members who made fun of me or called me a heroin addict.

"I will not allow anyone to harm you," he said. Because I'd feared men my whole life, I found it unusual that I was being protected and looked after first by the male nurse and now by the male guard. I believe they were living angels sent to me to calm my fear of men.

With the support of these two earth angels, I felt better. I started to eat better, and my gastrointestinal troubles improved. I began to gain weight again. Eight days later, I was practically a new person, and I was released.

I was overflowing with joy that I knew heaven was real.

After I was released, my daughter kept saying, "Mom, what happened? How could you be well? I don't understand."

I told her immediately, "I was healed. I was met by this giant white orb that I call the Great Glisten of the Eye of God."

Her eyes opened wide and all she could say was, "Wow." Then she said, "This is kind of strange, Mom." But she believed me.

For six months, it seemed that all I could do when I was alone was cry. When I was able to go to church again, the spiritual content of the lesson and the beautiful music were almost too much to bear. I learned to wear dark glasses and take lots of tissues. If anyone had asked why I was crying, I'm not sure I could have explained it. On one hand, I was grieving the loss of being in heaven; on the other, I was overflowing with joy that I knew it was all real and that I had experienced it firsthand. I only wished that I could have experienced the higher realm of heaven and that I could have stayed forever.

Processing the Experience

In addition to telling my daughter, I told close friends about my experience right away—not sharing it with them seemed unthinkable. Surely I had come back so that I could tell others not to be afraid of death. I had to share how filled I was with joy! They were incredibly supportive and urged me to tell my priest. I also found a support group for people who'd had near-death experiences. They helped me to understand that my experience was not an easy thing to process. The leader told me that, on average, it takes about seven years to come to grips with what happened. I found that to be true.

For me, the thing I wondered most was why I had come back. And what did God want me to do when I returned to earth? The voice I heard had said for me to continue to do what I'd been doing, but what did that mean?

One day about three years later, it just struck me. I was walking in my apartment, pondering it all, when I asked myself, "What have I been doing all my life?" The answer was suddenly so simple: prayer!

The Power of Prayer

After my accident, I had started feeling sorry for myself, and depression had set in. But the common thread of my entire life had been close contact with God, and the way to achieve that was prayer. Prayer is real. It is real power...the only power we have. If people only knew!

Once I realized how important prayer is and how it is the closest thing we have on earth to being in God's presence the way I had been, I wanted to tell everyone. I wanted to make sure that my daughter, especially, knew. She was my first thought in heaven: my love and my concern for her were the only things that still tied me to this earth. She believes every word of my experience, so if for no other reason, coming back was worth it just to be able to tell Mercedes.

Telling other family members has garnered mixed reviews. I find that many of them don't want to hear about what I witnessed. When

I tell them about the wisps of light that healed me, they become uncomfortable and quickly change the subject. I pray for them and leave them to God. But others, like my oldest brother, Frank, very much believe. My friends, especially the ones who convinced me to go to the priest about it, have been so accepting. They continue to be overjoyed with me. I only wish my entire family shared their enthusiasm.

I know that Jesus Christ is my best friend and that He is also my Savior.

I try not to let tepid receptions to my story bother me. I have faith that we will all come together because we were born into one another's lives with purpose. I learned that by being in heaven. I desperately want people to know what I experienced in heaven. People need to hear that there is something more, so my greatest joy here is to share what I've seen. Some may not want to believe, and that is their walk in life, but for me, I know that Jesus Christ is my best friend and that He is also my Savior. This is a mystery—that God can be both our best friend and our Savior, but only in Jesus Christ can it be true.

It took me a little over a year before I could walk long distances again. I started by walking to the park, then slowly adding two more blocks to the distance, then walking around the lake near my home. In two years' time, I could get into my car and drive again. I even rode a bike again! My daughter was having trouble with the brakes on her bicycle, so I said, "Let me test them for you," before I even thought about what I was doing. I rode a short distance on our quiet street and when I came back, Mercedes hugged me and reminded me that I hadn't ridden a bicycle since September 2003. I was almost in tears at the realization and overcome with joy.

After I was healed, I decided not to return to teaching. My doctor said going back into the highly stressful public school system would be a bad idea. She was amazed at my healing and said she couldn't believe it.

"Something extraordinary happened to you," she told me.

She was right! After returning from my adult near-death experience, my empathy was heightened even more than it had been after my childhood experiences with God. I found that I could feel everyone's feelings. If someone wasn't doing well, it was extremely difficult for me to deal with the empathy that overtook me.

I thought often about the message I'd been given at the gate of heaven: *Continue to do what you have been doing.* While I knew that prayer was a huge part of it, I also thought of the saints at the tables, directing human lives, providing opportunities for us to see signs of God.

I realized I needed to look for those signs in my own life. Now, whenever I see a sign that points toward unconditional love, allowing me to be of service to God, I follow that sign. That was the reason I returned to earth. The only thing that I'd ever done well in my life was keeping an open mind to forgiving others and, of course, praying. Always praying. Prayer, I have come to understand, is the answer to all things in my life.

Although I could not go back to the public school system, I found work again with special-needs people. I now teach meditation to disabled children and the elderly, as well as people with brain injuries. The key to my work is approaching each person with love. People have to feel love in order to respond properly and accept help. This was exactly what Jesus did for me when He came out of the giant white orb. He taught me to accept His love, and now I try to share that same love with others.

> *I know from my time in heaven that God breathes for us.*

I also teach private yoga, mostly to senior citizens in their homes. Through this work, I've helped offset dementia and calm tremors by teaching mindful breathing. I know from my time in heaven that God breathes for us, and when I see someone not breathing correctly, I can teach that person about this. I have a great affinity for the elderly. I've found that they tend to be the most open to hearing about my near-death experience, and they appreciate the help I can give.

Additionally, I have taken up painting and have learned to copy the masters, which has been a true joy to me. I feel that painting makes a certain sense to me that it wouldn't have before my time in heaven. Painting is all layers: each layer is beautiful and profound on its own, and the layers all work together to create the masterpiece. I think painting resonates for me because I see things differently now. I no longer see the regular air that we live in; I see and feel the air as a substance. I see the substance of light everywhere I look.

Also, when I paint, I can once again hear the sound of heaven. I hear the sound of heaven's music also when I help nonverbal children or those with profound disabilities. I can feel the cycle of rebounding love that constantly flows between all souls. It is the love of Jesus Christ.

Sharing My Story

After coming back from my adult near-death experience, I decided to tell the story of my childhood abuse. For years, I could not understand why I couldn't enter heaven's gates and why the sand and the road had moved and dipped when I'd asked about whether the abuse had been my fault. Now I have come to understand the meaning of it all. God was telling me not to fall into the quicksand of not telling my story. If I want to return to heaven, I have to open up and be honest about what happened to me. It is the only way to make peace with it all. If I keep it secret, it will take me like quicksand back into depression.

The first time I was open about my entire story publicly was when a university professor invited me to speak to his philosophy students about my near-death experience. The professor was teaching about death and dying, and he wanted me to share my story with his class. Before I was to speak to his students, the professor and I spoke at length. I told him about the shifting sand at heaven's gate and how I thought it was a message about not hiding the abuse. He was shocked to learn that I'd been through something of such magnitude, and he agreed that the abuse was integral to the story and urged me to tell my story in its entirety—except for one part.

He told me that I could not talk about Jesus as the way to heaven because it would alienate non-Christian students. The professor himself was not Christian. I refused this request, and I refused to speak to his class. I told him that Jesus was not only part of the story, but the crux of it all.

A few years later, the professor called and told me that he had just accepted Jesus into his life! It gives me great happiness for others to find that they, too, can call on God and Jesus. They are always with us if only we will go to them and open ourselves up to them. Their home is in our hearts, and that is why we can be filled with so much love. God wanted me back on earth to help others, to "continue to do what I had been doing." Serving humanity and sharing His love is our purpose. Every day of my life, I am aware that I live in two worlds: the world of heaven and the world of now.

> *God wanted me back on earth to help others.*

If I could get across just one main message, it would be that Jesus is our best friend. When I hear of people who are struggling in this life, it pains me to think that they are bearing their burdens alone when I know that God is so willing to comfort us.

Because they have seen my gift for empathy, friends will sometimes ask me to meet someone they know who is going through a hard time. Whenever I meet these people, the first thing I ask is, "Where are you in your prayer life? What kind of prayer life do you have?" The next questions are, "Do you believe that Jesus came as the Son of God? Do you believe that He healed and has all power?" It is astounding to realize that we have access to such unlimited capacity.

Jesus taught that if we have faith, we can move mountains, but we don't really fathom it. He came to show us our potential, but we seem to ignore it in the day-to-day, and we are so likely to let our power source go untapped. For me, personally, I devote four to six hours a day to prayer. I don't say this to brag about how spiritual I am; I share it only because I understand how important it is to me. Without that intense prayer time, I honestly do not believe I could function. Prayer is food for our souls, and perhaps because I have known what it means to be more fully in His presence, my soul starves for that time with the Lord.

It is much easier for me to be here now because I know where I am going. For me, knowing that heaven is there and that we serve an all-powerful God is everything. I see so much anxiety on this planet, but if others knew what I know, they could be free of this anxiety like I am. Having this awareness makes me want to share with others that Jesus is the Son of God and that we are all divinely created and loved. The intensity of my memories of my near-death experiences have in no way diminished. If anything, the intensity has only grown.

My Life since My Near-Death Experience

Alma Blasquez

I knew there was a reason for my return from my NDE, but I wasn't told what that was during the experience. I was simply told, "Continue to do what you have been doing."

Q *In reliving your NDEs, have you come to realize why God has given you a glimpse of heaven?*

A It took me years to process the messages I received about praying, love, and the connectedness of all people. I now understand that God was showing me that He loves us so much and that we must make the decision to come to Him. He has done all the work to reconcile us to Himself, but we have to reach out and accept His unconditional love and His grace.

My experiences allow me to authoritatively tell people that God is real and heaven is real because I've been there and I've seen it for myself. I want to urge other people to seek God and follow Him.

Q *What has been the biggest challenge in returning to an earthly life after your adult NDE?*

A My biggest grief has been seeing people who are suffering but will not accept that prayer is real. They don't understand that going to God is a must and that accepting Jesus as Lord and Savior is the answer. It hurts me to see so many people who do not want to be healed of their suffering. They think they are so bad inside that God could not possibly love them. I understand this because that was how I used to feel before my adult NDE; I, too, felt unlovable. But God showed me I was wrong, and my life changed when I accepted His love.

Q *What has been the biggest joy or surprise since returning to an earthly life after your NDEs?*

A The most delightful surprise of my adult life has been my angels coming back. I know they are still with me. They came back because I asked for them. Angels are real—more real than we can even think. Our cognition has to go away to allow this pure reality of heaven to be felt.

I did not expect my angels to be so active in my adult life, but they have shown up in incredible ways. They make me excited to tell people about Jesus. They keep me focused on what is to come.

Q *How have your feelings or the intensity of your feelings changed since your NDEs?*

A I hear a lot of people who have had NDEs say they came back with a peacefulness and deeper sense of love. Those feelings are true in my case as well, but one of the greatest gifts of my near-death experience has been the capacity to forgive. Now, forgiveness is a way of life for me—constant, like love.

The brief time I was in heaven, surrounded by those thousands of other souls, I could feel the connectedness of humanity. I suppose it also gave me a sense of the frailty of our human condition. Even though I have suffered terrible wrongs in my life, I have developed an intense ability to forgive others since I returned from the gate of heaven.

It may be hard for some people to understand how I could forgive those who abused me. It took me much prayer to understand that forgiveness does not mean excusing someone's behavior. In spite of it all, though, I know that we are supposed to forgive and learn. Forgiveness is what God gives us every day. If we only knew how much Jesus loves us and what it means to be forgiven by God Himself, I know we would live differently and try harder to forgive others the way God forgives us.

My near-death experiences have also given me great compassion and empathy. I know that the tenderness I feel for others comes from God. It comes from Jesus. Everything that I am comes from the Father, the Son, and the Holy Spirit. My purpose on this earth is to make their love known, to show it to others.

God blessed me with the empathy to feel what others are feeling— every anxiety, every hope, every dream—with the same intensity they feel it. It's almost as if I can go into someone else's heart and feel that person's entire soul, heart, and mind and then come back into myself. Sometimes this empathy can be overwhelming, knowing that I can somehow be part of someone else's being. The closer I am with the person, the more intense my empathy, but on some level, it is always there. When we forgive and seek connection with others, it opens us up to God's working in our life.

I am at peace, and I can feel throughout my body when others are not at peace. This is not a comfortable feeling for me, but I offer people reassurance that God is with them. I tell them things will be okay. I am the most authentic person I can be when I share this message because I know it is true.

This incredible sense of peace has led me to take up painting. I want to paint what I saw during my NDE and share with others the unimaginable beauty of the realms of heaven. I want to help people visualize the light effects of the diamonds on the ground and the shimmering of the waterfall because words can't describe the scene.

Q During your NDE, did you see glimpses of the future? If so, have those glimpses come true?

A Yes, I have had visions of the future since my NDEs began, but I don't talk about them a lot because I don't want to scare anyone. I began having nightmares about the end of the world when I was seven years old, but now I realize that the end will actually be a new beginning for those who love and trust in God.

Other times, I have had visions of things that have since come to pass. I had visions of my father's death and of my young daughter having a seizure before those things occurred. I saw a vision of the burning of the Amazon right after my adult NDE in 2000. To my amazement, it happened in 2019. I had kept that vision to myself except for telling a few close friends, who were just as amazed as I was when it occurred.

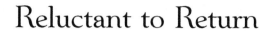

Reluctant to Return

By Jeffrey Coggins, as told to Ginger Rue

Open your eyes, look within.
Are you satisfied with the life you're living?

Bob Marley

I was supposed to be dead. That was the plan. So when I realized what was happening—that I was being escorted by angels to the heavenly realm—I was furious. I wanted to end it all, not start a new beginning. I just wanted everything to be over. Final.

At the ripe old age of nineteen, I thought I knew everything. Turns out, God had a lot He wanted me to learn.

A Storybook Childhood

Although I tried to end my life, I hadn't always been unhappy. I was born in 1970, the only child in a military family. During the first few years of my life, I lived in Germany, where the US Air Force stationed my dad until just after the end of the Vietnam War in 1975. My father and I were not close. He was a distant man, a genius with all things except social skills. He rarely said much, but when he did, it was usually profound. In fact, I wouldn't understand many of the things he told me as a child until I was in my thirties. Dad was a mobile communications technician during the war, and this meant that he was either always deployed or at a school in Greece or another country in that area. I rarely saw him when I was a child.

I learned a lot of Bible stories as a young child just through sightseeing.

Mom, however, was a secretary on the base, and the two of us were best friends. That didn't mean that Mom was a pushover by any means. Whenever I misbehaved and heard the click of her high-heeled shoes as she raced over to correct me, I straightened up quick!

Growing up in Germany in my early years was almost like growing up in a storybook land. The cobblestone roads, police officers riding Clydesdales, the beautiful old buildings, bells chiming three times a day—it was the perfect place to nurture childhood wonder as well as a sense of safety and calm.

We didn't go to church much for worship because Germany was primarily Lutheran, and we were Baptists. But Mom and I did visit lots of old churches in Germany, Switzerland, Sweden, and France, just to take in their beauty. We were more tourists than worshippers, but because most of the historic sites in Europe are unavoidably religious to some degree, I learned a lot of Bible stories as a young child just through sightseeing.

When I was in kindergarten, Mom decided it was time we went on another sightseeing adventure. "When I get off work on Friday, we're going to Versailles," she announced. It was a long way, and she was worried we wouldn't make it in time for the last tour, which was early in the evening. After rushing as best we could, we arrived just as the tour guide was ushering the last tour of the day inside the palace.

"Wait here," Mom told me. "I'm going to ask the tour guide if he'll let us join this last group."

While Mom walked a few feet away to speak to the tour guide, I noticed a bunch of ladybugs crawling around in a corner nearby. As I went closer to investigate, the ladybugs all took flight at the same time and began swarming around me, then landed on me, then quickly flew away. I wasn't frightened; the experience made me laugh. The tour guide who was talking to my mom noticed, and so did a priest from the palace chapel. The priest and the tour guide spoke to each other in French, which my mom could not understand. In English, the tour guide told my mom that we were going to be allowed into the chapel without the rest of the tourists.

"Be on your best behavior," Mom cautioned. Inside the chapel, the priest lit a candle. Then he extended his hand to me, and I shook it. They gave Mom a map of the grounds and told us we were free to walk around by ourselves as long as we liked.

Even though the tour guide never really explained our special treatment, Mom told me years later she'd gotten the feeling that maybe the priest viewed the ladybugs playing with me as some sort of sign—like maybe he thought the spirit of the former queen approved of me or something. I found out years later that in the Middle Ages, some Europeans believed that ladybug spots represented the Seven Sorrows of Mary after farmers prayed to Mary to save their crops from a plague of aphids and, shortly thereafter, a cloud of ladybugs appeared and ate the pests. Based on that legend, Europeans have always considered a ladybug landing on someone to be a good omen. Supposedly, it means good fortune will follow you or that someone is thinking of you.

I still don't understand the significance of that moment in my childhood. Sometimes I think God shows us things we won't understand until later in life. I do know that I saw that priest again years later in a very different setting.

Back in the States

We moved to the US after the Vietnam War ended, settling near Lubbock, Texas, in a little town called Wolfforth. What a big adjustment for me. I guess you could say I experienced culture shock.

Sometimes I think God shows us things we won't understand until later in life.

At only five years old, I suddenly found myself in a completely different world. In contrast to the storybook land of Europe with its beautiful churches and elaborate castles, the buildings in Texas were square, boxy, and seemingly identical, especially on an air force base.

More jarring than the scenery, though, was the difference in people. Americans seemed less gentle and gracious than Europeans. I was shocked at how rude other kids were. When the teacher introduced me to the class on my first day of school, the other kids stuck their tongues out at me. I was surprised when the teacher did not punish them for it. In Europe, children were not allowed to behave in such a way with impunity.

In spite of the rocky start, though, I found that it wasn't hard to make friends. As my newness wore off, the other kids seemed to like me.

I had a lot of friends but preferred quality over quantity. It was more important to me to have an inner circle I could trust than to be part of a large group.

The junior high and high school were combined in the same building, which made it easy for me to mature too quickly for my own good. I was dating girls who were already in high school before I was, and I was hanging around with older guys.

Mom and Dad were worried about my growing up too fast. They decided I needed something to occupy my free time, so they signed me up for karate and then tae kwon do. It worked to some extent. I became focused on martial arts almost to the exclusion of anything else. My extreme dedication meant that I advanced quickly—so quickly, in fact, that my instructor told me one day that he had nothing more he could teach me. Without martial arts as an anchor, I found myself adrift in the proverbial teenage wasteland.

By senior year, a guidance counselor told me I was missing a few credits and wouldn't graduate on time. I decided there was no way I was hanging around at school, so I dropped out and took my GED, which I passed easily. Suddenly I was no longer in high school. I had even more free time—a dangerous thing for a popular know-it-all teenager.

Wild and Reckless

Most of my close friends from high school ended up joining the military afterward, so I started hanging out with a whole different cast of friends—hippies and bikers who were into heavy drinking and smoking weed. One of these kids, a girl I'll call Holly, told me she liked me a lot, even though I was dating her friend. She seemed so into me that I decided to cut ties with her friend and gave all my attention to Holly.

Was I in love with Holly? No. But I trusted her, and trust was not something I took lightly.

Holly and I had been dating for only about a month when she started messing around with one of my biker friends. I'll call him Ted. Ted wasn't exactly an upstanding citizen, but I spent a lot of time with him and his mom, so in my mind, we were sort of this little false family. I had always thought of this group of friends as being like the James Gang, rebels of society. You've heard of "honor among thieves"? We weren't thieves, but I thought we had an understanding—that we had one another's backs.

One day I tried to call Holly for several hours, but her line was always busy. (This was the 1980s, when busy signals were a thing.) Finally, I became so frustrated that I decided to just go over to her house. She lived only about two miles away, so I walked. It was a hot August day in Texas, and when I arrived, Holly's window was open. She was on the phone with Ted, and I could hear her conversation. This already felt like a betrayal, because according to what I considered a universally understood "bro code," guys just didn't call their friends' girlfriends. I could've given them the benefit of the doubt until I heard Holly tell Ted she loved him. That did it.

Because the betrayal was simultaneously from both my friend and my girlfriend, I felt like I had not one, but two, knives in my back. I popped up where Holly could see me. I can't remember what I said to her, but she knew she'd been caught. She hung up on Ted and tried to pretend nothing was wrong.

"What's the matter?" she asked. When I told her what I'd heard, we argued. She tried to tell me they were just friends and that I'd misunderstood somehow, but she knew I could see right through her. I was young and brash, and she couldn't have reasoned with me at that point. I felt so foolish for having trusted Holly and Ted. Flooded with adrenaline, I just started running.

Looking back, I know it sounds kind of crazy to have gotten so upset over a friend like Ted and a girl I wasn't in love with and who I'd been dating for such a short time, but being impulsive is part

> *Being impulsive is part of youth, I guess.*

of youth, I guess. I felt betrayed. I hated the idea that people who had pretended to care about me had tricked me.

As I raced toward home, I decided that I didn't want to live in a world where people were so sneaky, a world where people were just users and abusers. And the more I thought about it, the more I felt that I'd never be able to trust anyone ever again.

Sometimes suicide attempts, especially among teenagers, can be a cry for help. That wasn't the case with me. I could hardly wait to get home and put an end to my life, to make sure I never had to feel anything ever again.

It just so happened that as I was running home, I ran right past a policeman. I guess seeing a nineteen-year-old guy running at that speed must've made him suspicious, so he stopped me. "Where are you going?" he asked.

"I'm going home," I replied.

"Let me see your ID."

I handed him my ID and took off running again. I didn't want anything to delay me.

With pills and alcohol in hand, I locked myself in the bathroom.

When I ran into the house, my dad was watching TV and my mom was doing the dishes. They paid no attention to me. I grabbed a bottle of Bacardi I'd stashed out of my parents' view. I went to the medicine cabinet, searching for every pill bottle I could find that had a warning label that the medicine could cause drowsiness and should not be taken with alcohol. I found an antihistamine and a strong muscle relaxant my mom sometimes took for her back pain.

With pills and alcohol in hand, I locked myself in the bathroom. I swallowed what was in the bottles, washing them down with the full bottle of Bacardi.

A little while later, my mom knocked on the bathroom door. I guess she must've heard the door slam and wondered what was wrong. When I wouldn't open the door, she broke in and found me on the floor, along with the empty alcohol and pill bottles. She dragged me into the living room. Just then the doorbell rang. It was the policeman who'd taken my ID; he'd come to the house to return it. Mom showed him the empty pill bottles and told him I'd taken them all at once. She had no idea how many pills had been in each bottle, so the police officer radioed for an ambulance. I started yelling at them both to leave me alone.

Everything seemed to be happening really fast. The next thing I knew, the ambulance arrived. But since I was nineteen, the EMTs couldn't take me to the hospital against my will unless I had passed out. I refused to go with them, so everyone just stood around until I was out cold. Then they took me.

Once I got to the hospital, I was in and out of consciousness for a while. I remember a nurse kept shaking me to wake me up. She told me I needed to take this medicine she was trying to give me or they'd have to pump my stomach. I was in no condition to be making decisions, and I didn't want any ultimatums. I couldn't speak, and I wasn't sure where I was. I felt like I was drifting away.

Out-of-Body Experience

All of a sudden, I didn't feel drunk or foggy at all. I felt as though I were slipping to the left off the hospital bed. I remember feeling like I needed to grab on to something so I could sit up and steady myself. As I tried to hold on to the bed, I felt like I was remembering something that had never happened to me. I saw a pretty house, a nice car, and a family, but none of them was mine. I'd never seen them before. And yet it somehow felt like a memory.

Immediately I fell back down onto the bed. I opened my eyes and saw a doctor standing over me, trying to resuscitate me. I tried to sit up again, thinking that the doctor would move out of my way, but he didn't. The next thing I knew, I was inside the doctor's mind and was seeing things from his perspective. The family, the house, and the car I had seen moments before were his. I could also feel what he was feeling: panic. The vision overwhelmed and repelled me. I slammed back onto the bed.

Soon I felt myself slipping to my left again. I looked to my right and saw my own body next to me. I saw a flash of blue light come from behind the doctor over to my right. Then I noticed a large column of light in the corner of the room.

> *They looked like storybook fairies, but now I define them as angels.*

I heard a voice from the light say, "It's all right; we'll save you." I looked more closely at the blue light. It looked like a little fairy in the moon in a children's storybook. The blue fairy took me by the hand.

Next, I saw a glimmer of green light come out of the large column of light. I could not see the green light as clearly as I had seen the blue one. It seemed that the green light made an effort to keep me from seeing her by pulling my arm up over my head and behind me in a way that spun me around upright. I can't really explain why, but somehow I felt that both lights were female presences. The blue one was a dark-haired girl with tan skin, and for some reason, I think the green one was blond, though I'm not sure why since I never saw her clearly. I had only a fleeting glimpse as she rushed at, then by me. At the time, both looked to me like storybook fairies, but now I define them as angels.

The two lights pulled me upright and off to the right side of the room in the corner, behind the doctor. I snatched my hands away from them, unsure of what was happening. I wanted to see what was going on. I could see everyone and everything in the room: the doctor, the crash cart next to him, all the medical equipment, and nurses scrambling here and there. The doctor was trying to revive me. I saw one of the nurses put an oxygen mask over my face. I was scared and confused. Things were happening faster than I could process.

I noticed that my dad was not there, which did not surprise me in the least. He had become disabled a few years after we returned to the States, and he had trouble walking. His immobility had made the distance between him and others even greater, and his overarching parenting philosophy had always been that parents should stand back and let children learn from their own mistakes.

I saw my mom standing in the doorway with her arms folded, a worried look on her face. As a military wife from the Vietnam age, Mom was not a woman prone to hysterics, but I could tell she was working hard to hold it together. She moved out of the way as another nurse came rushing into the room.

The green angel said, "We don't have time for this. We have to go. We have to hurry." She seemed annoyed with me. I was just beginning to realize that I was dead.

The angels grabbed me and pulled me into the large column of light. Inside the light was a tunnel. I couldn't keep my eyes open long because I began to feel queasy, as if I was on a carnival ride. But every once in a while, I would open my eyes and see a kaleidoscope of color, as well as a variety of other things, shooting past me at a high speed.

I saw a stairway next to a platform-like area. I'd heard the term "stairway to heaven" and wondered if this was it. A man and his dog were standing next to it, just about to start walking up. The man was old with gray hair, Caucasian, and wearing a gray sweater. His dog was a collie who looked like Lassie. The man was hunched over slightly and was walking toward the stairs as fast as he could, which wasn't very fast. It was as though the dog was trying to lead him up the stairs. I saw them for only a split second. Then the image vanished.

I closed my eyes again. Even with my eyes closed, I could tell that light was flickering around me.

Destination Reached

After what seemed like a couple of minutes, I opened my eyes again and saw just clouds, like in the night sky. I looked over my shoulder and saw the biggest crowd of people I'd ever seen in my entire life—an unbelievable number. The people were standing in front of a big wall that I assumed to be the gate of heaven. The angels dropped me down in the middle of the crowd, and I thought I would never get to the front to see what was going on.

Knowing about Jesus and the Bible and having faith are two different things.

Just then I saw that other little angels were flying around above us, picking people up and taking them over the wall. Two of them came right to me and picked me up. When they set me down, I was over the wall, kneeling with my eyes closed. Upon opening my eyes, I saw that I was in what looked like a thick cloud that opened into a room. The walls of the room were made of clouds about twenty-five feet tall. I wasn't sure where I was, but I knew I didn't like it.

This is not dead, I remember thinking. *And I am not happy.* Angrily, I walked over to one of the cloud walls, thinking I would just walk through it. Something or someone told me, "Don't do it. You'll regret it. The wall is greedy. You'll be lost forever." It wasn't just a voice; it was multiple communications at once. I could hear the words, but I could also feel the words and the emotions behind them from the speaker of the words. I was so shocked that I can't even say whether the voice was male or female, but I felt a sense of doom as an image of me falling to earth flashed before me.

The image frightened me into submission, but I was still angry. I suppose that I was so young and arrogant that I thought my suicide would lead me into nothingness. I was not prepared for there to be an afterlife. I was well versed in Christianity, as well as many other religions, but I had studied them more on an academic level than out of a search for truth. I had read the entire New Testament by the age of twelve or thirteen, plus a good bit of the Old Testament as well. When my parents had enrolled me in karate classes, my teacher had taken the body, mind, and soul approach: He felt that it wasn't enough to just learn a bunch of moves. He wanted me to understand the meanings, history, philosophy, and art of those moves. As a result, I knew a good bit about Buddhism, too, but I viewed it as more of a science tied to martial arts than a religion.

Likewise, although I had a general understanding of Christianity, I was not a religious guy. Knowing about Jesus and the Bible and actually having faith are two entirely different matters. I certainly wasn't spending my Sunday mornings in Bible class. In fact, Sunday mornings I most likely would be sitting on the porch, wondering what I'd done the night before or what had happened to my car.

Spoiled and cocky as I was, as I stood in the cloud room, my first impulse was to complain.

"So this is heaven," I said mockingly. "At least they could have given me a bench or something to sit on!" Just then a marble bench appeared before me. But was I grateful? No. "Great," I said. "A marble bench.

I bet it's going to be cold." But when I sat down on it, it wasn't cold. Then a corner of the room turned flat. The clouds darkened and began to swirl. One of the cloud walls opened like an elevator door, and three figures stood before me, silhouetted by a bright light. Not only could I see them, but I could also feel them. One of them was my grandmother.

One of the cloud walls opened, and three figures stood before me.

An old lady I didn't know was on one side of her. "See, I told you so," the old lady said to my grandmother. What that meant, I still do not know. Maybe she meant, "I told you he'd make it to heaven after all," or maybe she meant, "I told you he wouldn't be happy to be here."

The third figure was a young girl who looked to be about thirteen or fourteen years old. She was wearing an old-fashioned-looking white gown, like one you would see on a young girl from prairie days. Full of exuberance, she flew into the room with a joyous squeal and sat down next to me on the bench. The door closed, and my grandmother and the old lady were gone.

"What happened?" the young girl asked me. I'd never been one to share my problems with others, especially strangers, but she did not seem like a stranger to me. I felt like I had known her my whole life without being aware of it. I felt that her purpose always had been to help me and that she had somehow guided me through difficulties I'd faced. I could tell she was wise beyond her youthful appearance, and she also seemed to be filled with compassion and caring.

After I told her my story, she took me on several journeys.

Far from Heaven

In what felt like a personalized retelling of *A Christmas Carol*, the young girl took me first on a journey to my past. She showed me significant moments I remembered where I'd done things that had impressed people, and she also showed me things people had said about me that I never knew. She showed me people who had been affected by my life and who would be affected by my death. Then she showed me things that were relevant while I was in the hospital— people who were worried about me, people I wouldn't have suspected would care.

Finally, she showed me some scenes from the future, but those scenes lasted the least amount of time because the future is always changing. She explained that the only things in the future that could not be changed were the consequences of past actions. Even though she showed me the past, present, and future, sadly, at nineteen I was too selfish and arrogant to really care about any of it.

On the next journey, I could not see the young girl with me. On some level, I felt that she was there whether I could see her or not. But presumably alone, I woke up in a grassy field on a sunny day. It was like waking up somewhere after a big New Year's Eve party and wondering where I was and what in the world had happened the night before. I wondered if this was the end. I didn't feel intoxicated or dreamy; in fact, I felt extremely clearheaded. I started wondering if maybe this was heaven. But all too soon, I realized that could not be the case.

I heard totally unappealing voices. The voices belonged to a girl and two guys. Even though I'm from the South and am used to hearing southern accents, there are different types. I'll just say these voices did not use the lovely, languid dropping of *R*s. I could hear the guys and the girl laughing. I was in no mood to be around anyone, and certainly not them. I tried to quietly and slowly get up to look over the grass so I could see who they were. I wanted to get a peek at them without their seeing me.

The first thing I saw was a run-down old shack. A breeze blew across the grass, and I caught a whiff of the foulest smell. It smelled like skunk and sewage and other rancid things mixed together. I saw the people I'd heard talking, but they weren't really people. They were wearing overalls and had human bodies, but their faces were those of jackals.

Trying to elude their notice was like trying to sneak around a junk-yard dog; they immediately spotted me and came running over. They asked who I was and where I'd come from. I say they "asked," but when they communicated with me, they communicated in various forms. Words weren't necessary. I didn't respond to them. All of a sudden, one of them pointed to the sky.

I looked up and saw a large crack appear in the sky and then rip open, like a piece of paper being torn in half. A giant, brown crea-ture jumped out of the opening and landed next to me. I think it had decided that I wasn't going to fall for whatever it was these jackal-faced "people" had planned, so he decided to take care of me himself.

The creature had six eyes and horns all over his head. He was cussing violently. Oddly, he was not like a creature in a scary movie, but more like a cartoon. I think he appeared in this way because that was the only way I could conceive of him. It was like a child's idea of a scary monster. He was a foul creature and smelled rank, and although I was no stranger to bad language from my association with bikers, his profanity-laced rant was hard even for me to listen to. Nothing came out of his mouth except for curses and insults. He grabbed me and jumped back into the hole in the sky.

We landed on a crescent-shaped platform in space, with a wall of what looked like television screens that were shaped more like cubes than flat surfaces. In each cube, people were being shown in different terrifying situations.

> *The creature derived a sick joy from watching people suffer.*

Some were running from animals; others were covered in spiders. The creature pointed to a control panel that he operated. He told me this was hell, and that every cube was a custom-made hell for every doomed soul.

Hell, he explained, was ever changing: once people adapted to a certain form of misery and built up any tolerance to the torment, their hell was immediately changed to provide fresh horrors. Once they became used to a certain type of pain, a new pain was introduced.

The people in the cubes could never predict what type of evil they would face next. The creature derived a sick joy from watching people suffer. Each person's hell, I came to understand, was unique to them.

As I walked along the wall of cubes, I was suddenly sucked into one of them. I found myself in a small, white room with nothing but a door and a shelf. Soon the door opened, and a guy and a girl walked in. These were not the jackals from the grassy field; they were both very good-looking. They were almost like twins. Both were extremely nice to me and asked if they could get me anything.

I'd never been one to eat and drink in strange places or with people I didn't know; I always had to feel comfortable in order to relax enough to enjoy food or drink. For that reason, I kept saying no to their offers. However, they kept insisting, so I finally agreed to a sandwich and a Coke.

I realized this had been my own private cube of torture.

The two of them left the room and came back with the sandwich and Coke and set them on the shelf in front of me. I was skeptical, so I didn't touch the plate or the glass.

"Come on," they kept saying. "Take a bite and enjoy!" After a great deal of urging on their part, I inspected the sandwich to make sure it was what I thought it was; I finally gave in and took a bite. Immediately I was repulsed by the rancid flavor. I spit the food out of my mouth and grabbed the soda to wash out the taste, but the soda was just as bad, so I spit it out too. The guy and the girl laughed hysterically at me. Then they apologized and offered to get me another sandwich and drink.

"No, thanks," I said.

They started trying to convince me that they'd just been joking the first time and that it wouldn't happen again, but I refused to listen. After I got tired of the back and forth, I just stopped talking to them altogether. I began to see that these two good-looking young people were not what they had first appeared to be. They were not attractive or even human at all. They were like the jackals in the field, only a mask was covering their faces. I was suddenly able to see through the masks as though they were transparent.

I realized that this had all just been my own private cube of torture and that the creature who had shown me the cubes was not just a
monster, but none other than the devil himself. He could see inside me
just like Jesus could see inside me. He knew my greatest fears were not
spiders or snakes or darkness or fire. My fear was people deceiving me.
These jackal-faced people who'd tricked me and laughed at me were just
like people in the real world, and the situation I was in with them was
very much like the one that had led me to commit suicide. This is a message, I realized. People can seem to be one way, but they are really just
jackals. God is telling me that people are not what they appear to be.

I remembered an old Greek fable I'd learned in school about a
young woman who'd been taken into the underworld. Her name was
Persephone, and she'd been tricked into eating something that would
force her to stay in the underworld forever. I'd hated English class and
had never paid much attention to my teacher's lessons, but now I was
starting to think how wise she had been to teach us something like
that. I wondered if maybe the boy and girl had kept trying to get me to
consume something because if they could trick me into swallowing the
food or drink, they'd be able to keep me there forever.

Just as I was processing all this, a sudden whirlwind whisked me up
and snatched me out of the cube. As I left the platform, I could hear the
devil screaming, "No!"

The next thing I knew, I was shown flashes of all the bad things I
had ever done. But it wasn't simply a life review. In these flashes, I was
put into other people's consciousness as I was doing the bad things to
them. I could feel the way I'd made them feel. I saw and felt how insen-
sitive I had been without even realizing it. I had never known how often

I'd said something hurtful without even being aware of it. For example, in one scene, I was sitting around drinking with a friend of mine, and

It was excruciating to relive moments I had forgotten about.

a large woman had walked by. I made some crack about her weight—something I forgot two seconds after I'd said it. But what I hadn't known was that this friend of mine had an overweight mother, and my comment had cut him to the bone.

It was excruciating to relive moments like this that I had forgotten all about or hadn't cared about in the first place. I felt desperation upon realizing that there was so much I could have done differently—better—if only I'd had better perspective during my life. I'd lived in such a myopic way, but now that I was forced to step back and see things I'd never seen before, I felt terrible about myself and was overwhelmed by a feeling of cold. I shivered uncontrollably as my eyes filled with tears.

Many years later, I learned that Jesus had told His followers that "everyone will have to give account on the day of judgment for every empty word they have spoken." (Matthew 12:36, NIV) Having had a small taste of this, I can say firsthand that this should be one of the most sobering warnings in all the Bible. It was truly agonizing to feel what I had made others feel with my careless words.

The Pit of Purgatory

After enduring all this, I felt something shift. I knew instinctively that the flashes of the past were over and that I had been put down somewhere new. I opened my eyes and saw that I was in a hole—a cave of some kind. Of all the places I went, this horrible place was the one I remember most vividly.

The ceiling was low, the floor was cold and wet, and I was surrounded by darkness. I felt alone and abandoned. I tried to move through the darkness of the cave, but as I crawled around, I became wetter and colder, and I could not stand because the ceiling was so low. I could not sit down either. I couldn't position myself in any way that was comfortable. But the physical discomfort was not the real problem.

When I say I felt abandoned, I mean that it was an intense feeling of separation from God. It was strange because I had never really had a strong relationship with God, but now I was acutely aware of being without Him. I liken this sense to sitting in a room with the light on but never noticing the light until someone suddenly switched it off. Think of those moments in movies when someone realizes he has lost the great love of his life and there's nothing he can do about it—that feeling of hopelessness. Imagine that times a thousand. I realized in that moment that no one would ever love me more than Jesus did, and I'd rejected Him, and now it was too late.

I was trapped in a wretched place, looking at my life and facing all the horrible things I'd done. I'd never appreciated what a gift it was to be alive, and I'd been willing to throw it all away. I realized that I'd wanted out of my life so much that I'd chosen a permanent solution to a fixable problem. Now, however, this situation was unfixable. In my earthly life, I'd had options. Here, I had none. There was nothing I could do.

Ahead of me, I saw an amber light. I hoped that it might offer some warmth, so I crawled toward it as best I could. As I got closer, I saw that other people were near the light, all kneeling at the side of an opening. I could see that there was a fire inside this hole.

The people near the fire were terrifying. One was a girl with cut, bleeding wrists; another was a man with a rope around his neck; still another was a man with the back of his head blown out from a gunshot; others were hollow-eyed girls who looked like they'd overdosed on pills or heroin. Like me, they had all died from suicide. I could hear screaming coming from the hole of fire.

"Where am I?" I asked the others.

"Be quiet or you'll be next!" one of them hissed.

Just then a huge, ugly demon reached out of the hole and grabbed someone and dragged that person down into the fire. I was filled with terror that I would be next. As I knelt down and closed my eyes, I became overwhelmed again with visions of all the bad things I had done in my life, once again acutely feeling the pain I had so casually caused others to feel.

I opened my eyes to stop the visions from coming. As I looked around, I saw that all the other souls in the cave looked like wide-eyed zombies. They could not close their eyes either, without seeing their own hurtful behavior. *This is purgatory*, I thought. We could not close our eyes, and we could not talk to one another. We could not stand up. We could not sit down. We could only kneel there on the tips of our toes and the points of our knees. All we could do was stare at the hole of fire, listen to the screams, and hope we would not be next.

Ahead of me, I saw a pudgy man in a tattered gray robe. The man looked about forty years old and had a trimmed beard and a balding head like a monk. He was cleaner than the rest of the people there, which led me to believe he had been some type of religious figure, maybe a priest. But why would a priest be in purgatory with people who'd committed suicide? Then it crossed my mind: I wondered if he might be Judas, sent here for betraying Jesus. I knew, after all, that Judas had also committed suicide.

My eyes had been open for so long and were burning so badly that I didn't think I could take it anymore. I thought it might be worth it to see the horrible flashes of memories if only I could close my eyes for just a brief second. As I closed my eyes and the flashes of my evil ways rushed into my mind, I began to sob quietly. I thought, *I would do anything if I could just have another chance to go back because now I know how to fix it all. I would forgive people who hurt me. I would never take my own life. I would make sure to do everything right if only I could do it over again.*

Like a butterfly emerging from its cocoon a little at a time, I was experiencing a spiritual transformation.

The circumstances and the people who'd hurt me in my life seemed so inconsequential now. The incident with Holly and Ted that I'd taken so hard never even crossed my mind the entire time I was out of my body. In the scheme of things, it just didn't seem to matter. Like a butterfly emerging from its cocoon a little at a time, I was experiencing a spiritual transformation.

Then I heard a female voice say, "If you ask Him, maybe He will save you." I'm not sure if it was the little girl who served as my guide or a different voice, but I was so thankful to hear her speaking to me, especially with this message of hope. I wondered how it could be possible to be saved from this dreadful place.

I heard the voice again: "Say it. Say the words, 'Jesus Christ, my Savior in heaven, please save me.'" I said the words aloud. Then the

voice said, "Again." So I repeated the words over and over again: "Jesus Christ, my Savior in heaven, please save me!" The flashes stopped, and the screaming around me stopped. All was silent.

I thought, This must be an angel of the Lord.

Before the Throne

As I opened my eyes and looked up, I found that I was no longer in the cave. I was kneeling on another platform in space. Before me was a man sitting in a giant, stone chair. He looked, to me, like Jesus, with long brown hair, a robe, and candles surrounding Him—just like all the paintings I'd ever seen of Him. I don't know if what I saw was the way Jesus actually looks, but He was presented to me in a way that I could recognize Him.

To His right was an approximately six-foot-tall, silver winged creature that appeared to be female. It was hard to say for certain whether the figure was male or female, but I will call the figure "she."

Like the cartoonish embodiment of the devil I'd seen earlier, this figure was almost overdrawn in aspect, but at the same time, very real. She seemed to have no hair and was wearing a silver, winged helmet and shoes with wings, just like I'd seen in depictions of the Greek messenger god Hermes. She was holding a trident like the Greek god Poseidon. She wasn't standing but, instead, hovering just above the ground with her knees bent. I thought, *This must be an angel of the Lord.* She never faced me. I saw her only in profile as she looked over her shoulder at me. She was facing away from Jesus.

To the left of Jesus was a woman with three very old men behind her. I realized that the woman was Mary. Whether it was Mary the mother of Jesus or Mary Magdalene, I wasn't sure, but I somehow knew that her name was Mary and that she was special to Jesus.

The men behind her looked like the *Ten Commandments* movie version of Moses. I supposed them to be Abraham, Moses, and Peter or perhaps Paul or other important figures from the Bible. Every one of them had the same long beard and long hair. There was not much light around them, but I could see them clearly on the platform in their gray, brown, and tan robes. I could not be sure if there were more than three men because the area behind Jesus where they stood was lost in darkness.

We seemed to be somewhere in space. I looked up and saw lights that looked at first like stars. I realized they weren't stars at all—they were eyes, all looking at me. I could feel the presence of everyone in the room as well as those looking down from above. Because I could feel what every-one else felt, I realized that I knew some of the souls who were looking down on me. Some were my grandparents and other deceased relatives. I could not see them, but I knew that some of those eyes were theirs.

I could feel the disappointment of everyone who was looking at me. I could feel their outrage at what I had done with my life; I could feel the disapproval they had for all the unjustified things I'd ever said. The shame I felt from their disappointment was hard to bear.

Next, I looked at Jesus's face, and He did not look happy with me either. He, too, looked angry and disappointed. As much as I'd felt guilty under the gaze of everyone else there, the way Jesus looked at me cut me to my very soul. I'd never felt so ashamed.

As I've explained, in these realms, communication is more than just spoken words. I felt everyone around me and absorbed their emotions.

I felt everyone around me and absorbed their emotions.

I can only compare it to being in a pitch-dark room with someone else—the way you can feel that person even when you can't see that person. But besides just feeling someone's presence, I could feel their emotions too. The effect was overwhelming.

Feeling Jesus's disappointment in me was more than I could take in. I began to cry uncontrollably. Everyone was looking at me, and all I could do was sob. The tears in my eyes made it hard to see clearly, but I could not stop. It hurt me to know that I had hurt Jesus.

My sobbing was interrupted when the angel of the Lord spoke.

"Tell our Lord what brings you here," the angel said. I started trying to explain my suicide and the reason for it—how I'd felt that the world was unfair and I didn't want to be a part of it anymore. Jesus looked at me as if shocked by my complaints and my complete foolishness.

"Who told you it was going to be a fair world?" He asked audibly.

The Hall of Council

I didn't know how to reply to Jesus's question. Suddenly the young girl from the cloud room swooped in and whisked me away to a dark, large hall and put me in front of large double doors.

"Where are we?" I asked her.

"I have something to show you," she replied.

The doors opened, and about a dozen people walked out. One of them seemed vaguely familiar to me, but I could not place him. I knew him from somewhere, but where? I realized he was the priest I had met at Versailles when I was a child. I had forgotten he even existed. I had a brief flashback of that experience with the ladybugs. The room emptied, and the young girl and I went inside.

Inside the dark room was a huge round table with a three-dimensional display of the universe. The girl brought me to an old man sitting at the table. The man was bald and did not seem to be very tall, maybe standing only about five foot six. I would guess he would have weighed about 170 pounds.

Although the room was not well lit, illuminated only by the display of our galaxy above the round table, it looked to me like the man was about seventy-five years old. He was wearing a dark-brown robe. I don't know exactly who he was, but I could tell he was an elder. He seemed cranky and bothered by the interruption. He asked me, "Why are you here?"

"He feels that he was treated badly in his life and that it was unfair," the girl answered for me.

I could tell by his response that he found this preposterous, and so did the girl. That same acute level of empathy still allowed me to feel the emotion behind words, while also feeling what everyone else nearby was thinking about what the person had said. I could feel not only his emotions but hers as well.

At that point, I still was not sure where I was exactly, but I have come to think of this great room with the display of the universe as the "hall of council." It was not in heaven per se, because Jesus was not there. Only when I was in the presence of Jesus was I in heaven. Even in the cloud room where I'd been placed earlier, the kingdom of heaven was hidden from me. I believe this is because it is very hard to leave heaven, and if I had been allowed to see more of it, it would have been even harder for me to leave. I think the heavenly beings did not want to encourage me to want to stay.

Jesus replied, My son, I can heal those who are broken.

The old man started to explain things to me, but I could tell he did not want to. I could tell he saw me as a nuisance and resented my taking up his time. Still, he began to explain that the globe on the table was the universe.

"All the stars have meaning, and their arrangements have meaning," he said. He explained something about how when people are born, the arrangement of the stars in the universe influences the life they will lead. He explained that heaven is a safe place where souls are protected and taken care of by the Lord. He said that a person's status in heaven is based on what that person did and learned in the earthly world.

Deep down, I understood what he had said. Even so, none of the things I had experienced yet while journeying through this unknown realm had fully humbled me.

At Jesus's Feet

The next thing I knew, I could no longer see the little girl who had guided me. I was back on the platform before Jesus.

"What do you think of what you have learned?" Mary asked me.

Now that I'm older, I can't believe how I responded and what a brash young kid I was. The thoughts I'd had in purgatory about doing anything for another chance, about forgiving people and having better perspective, vanished so quickly. I'd been asked a question, and I replied with what felt like the honest answer.

"I think it's not right that I had to put up with people hurting me on earth," I responded. "Jesus was supposed to protect me, and if I'm going to go back, I want Him to make it right."

Jesus replied, "My son, I cannot cause pain to another. I can only heal those who are broken."

With the brashness of youth, I demanded to speak directly to God the Father.

"I want to see God!" I said.

I could feel how shocked they all were—the people in the room and the witnesses whose eyes I could see in the sky. They couldn't believe what I'd just said. Even with all the sadness and shame I felt, I still had warring emotions inside me. My earthly arrogance had not disappeared.

"You cannot see God!" Mary said angrily.

"No one can see God," Jesus said.

"Kneel down before the Great Healer and ask for forgiveness!" Mary instructed me.

Reluctantly, I knelt down. I could feel the great disappointment and astonishment at my audacity from the people in the room. I began to weep.

"Do you know why I saved you from the pit of purgatory?" Jesus asked me.

"No," I replied.

"Remember the old man? The one you thought was Judas? This showed me that you believe, that you truly believe."

I realized that Jesus saw something in me that I did not see in myself.

Although I had not lived my life for Jesus, if I hadn't believed in Him deep down, it never would have crossed my mind that the man I saw in purgatory was Judas. This proved that I believed the story of Jesus to be true. I'd seen the devil and recognized him for who he was, so how could I believe in the devil and not believe in Jesus? I had a tiny bit of faith in my heart. All I had to do was make it grow.

It was then that I realized that Jesus had been with me the whole time in that cave and that He had always been with me throughout everything that had ever happened to me in my life. I realized, too, that Jesus saw something in me that I did not see in myself. I continued to sob uncontrollably, kneeling on the floor with my head in my hands.

I had tried to kill myself because I was tired of living in a world where people just deceived one another. I hadn't realized that the world I'd lived in was the world I had made for myself. I was the one who had chosen the people I'd surrounded myself with. I'd just been too young and foolish to realize it. My life was a recipe for which I'd chosen the ingredients. If I didn't like the final result, I would have to change the recipe.

"Come forward and kiss His feet," Mary instructed me.

My body felt like it was weighed down with cement blocks on my back. By earthly measurements of time, I would estimate that it took me about five minutes to crawl only about five feet.

When I finally reached Jesus's feet, I was shocked by their appearance. They were dirty and worn, like you would expect from a man who'd walked in sandals for thirty-three years of life on earth. I was repulsed. *Isn't it just like God to do things differently than humans would expect?* I thought. Besides, God is God: He did not have to do things in a way that suited me. Kissing His feet was a way to show that I recognized that. I could humble myself and kiss Jesus's feet, or I could be doomed, so the choice was easy: I kissed them.

After I kissed Jesus's feet, I could feel myself being pulled back to the material world.

"No!" I cried out. "I want to stay!"

Jesus responded, "Give me a chance to make it right in the end." It was strange to me how things shifted from me humbling myself to Jesus to His asking me for something. I can only think this illustrates how Jesus is not only our King but also our Friend, how He loves us so much.

Still, I didn't like the idea that things wouldn't be fixed until "the end." Did that mean I would return to a messed-up life that would be fixed only right before I died?

"When will the end come?" I asked.

Mary said the number "forty-six." Then she gave me a compressed message in words, pictures, and emotions all rolled into one. She showed me a vision of future events that no one on earth could have predicted, many of which have come true since my return, including difficult times I would personally face. The message was brief, and the events were not put into context. It was more like seeing a series of photographs without knowing the stories behind them. I saw jobs I would have, people I would meet.

I thought the number forty-six would be the age when I would die, but I turned forty-six several years ago and am obviously still here, so I can't be certain about the significance of that number and why Mary said it to me, although I have pondered the question for decades.

I did not want to go back to earth. No one ever wants to go back.

As I went out the door, I once again entered a tunnel. At the end of the tunnel, I saw a vision of a turning circle with an eye in the middle. As the circle turned, I could see scenes around it like a clock of people and places, all moving at once. I realized that this circle was God and that He had allowed me to see Him in a form that I could understand. It was a great comfort to be given that image, even though Jesus Himself had said that I could not see God. The same feeling I'd had when I realized that Jesus had always been with me I now had from God Himself. It was as though He wanted to make sure I knew that He had been a part of everything I'd experienced.

I did not want to go back—no one ever wants to go back to earth, where we feel hot or cold or hungry or alone or in pain—but with this feeling of comfort, I submitted and went back peacefully. I remember thinking, *I will do whatever You want.*

Back to Life

As I entered my body again, I could feel my heartbeat. I noticed that my body felt uncomfortable from having lain in the same position for a long time. I was cold and hungry, sensations I had not felt outside my body. I could not communicate with anyone and remained in a coma for three days after returning. It was like I lived somewhere halfway between being asleep and awake. I could not move and I could not see. Even when I opened my eyes, everything was blurry.

As I lay there unable to move, I replayed the events in my mind over and over again so that I would be able to remember them later. Already, I could feel parts of the experience slipping away from me. I wanted to retain all I could.

At some point, I felt a small, warm hand in mine and struggled to open my eyes to see whose it was. I could make out the blurry silhouette of a young girl with dark eyes and long, straight brown hair standing next to my bed and looking down at me. She did not look like the young girl from heaven, and I could not feel her emotions the way I could with the other girl, but she still felt familiar and safe. She seemed a little older than the other girl too. This one seemed to be an older teenager or a woman in her early twenties. When I came out of the coma, I described the girl to the nurse, asking who she was and where she had gone.

"There were no young girls in the intensive-care unit," the nurse said. "No one has been allowed beyond the glass in three days. The only people who've been in here have been the same four women on twelve-hour shifts. But we're all older and have been working at the hospital for many years."

At first, I thought maybe it had all been a dream.

But then the nurse told me that at a point during my three days in intensive care, I had died for a full six minutes.

Lingering Effects

As soon as I came out of the coma, I was put on an elevator and taken to the hospital's psychiatric ward. I was informed that because of my suicide attempt, it was mandatory that I undergo a seventy-two-hour psychiatric evaluation.

God put me in situations where I had one of two choices: faith or no faith.

Being in a psych ward was quite a jolt back to reality. People were screaming and crying and running around and having all sorts of meltdowns. And once I was conscious, the doctors did not give me a lot of time alone with my thoughts. They promptly put me on a schedule and told me when I could leave my room, when I would eat dinner, when I would go to therapy, and when I would take my medications.

In spite of all this, I think the spirit of the little girl somehow stayed with me while I was there. I could clearly remember the sound of her voice, and to this day, I still hear it every now and again. Because of her, while I was in the hospital, I found myself taking the time to really listen to the other people in the ward, to help them however I could. I think the thing that changed me the most from the near-death experience was the memory of feeling how I had made others feel in the past. I suppose it would have been impossible for that not to have affected me.

I was a patient in the psych ward for a few weeks, which gave me some time to think about what had happened to me. While I was there, I tried to treat other patients the way the little girl in heaven had treated me, by listening and helping me understand that problems can be fixed.

I realized a lot of people would dismiss my experience as having been just a dream or a hallucination from the drugs and alcohol, but I knew better. I had been intoxicated on enough occasions to know that what

I experienced was not the result of that. And in dreams, I'd always been able to control what happened, to guide my dreams to a certain degree. In my near-death experience, I had no control, so it couldn't have been a dream. No, this had been something entirely different.

I think God made a believer of me because I let Him. He put me in situations where I had only one of two choices: faith or no faith.

So here's the part where I'm supposed to say that I turned my whole life around. That would probably make a better story, but the truth is, directly after getting out of the hospital, in spite of everything I'd witnessed, in spite of every promise I'd made, the second I had the opportunity, I jumped right back into my old life. I didn't tell anyone about what I'd experienced. I was afraid that if I went around saying I'd seen Jesus, people would think I was crazy, and I certainly didn't want to spend any more time in the psych ward.

Business as Usual

My parents and I didn't talk much about my suicide attempt. Neither lectured me about what I'd done. My dad was his usual stoic self, without much to say. Mom would come in and ask how I was doing and if I needed anything, but beyond that, we didn't have any deep discussions, and I didn't volunteer my afterlife experience.

As for Holly and Ted, neither of them came to the hospital. I decided to leave Holly and Ted to God and not worry about them anymore.

Sadly, I still had an expectation that life was supposed to be some sort of fantasy, one with lots of excitement and admiration.

I got deeper into a life of drugs and alcohol, fast cars, and playing pool. Five years later, I owned a four-bedroom house and three cars and had two different girlfriends and plenty of money. Lots of people wanted to hang out with me. I had the life I thought I wanted. So why did I feel so empty? I realize now that God sometimes gives us what we ask for just to show us that it's not what we think it is. Be careful what you wish for, as the saying goes.

> *I knew I was an alcoholic, and I knew I needed to change my life.*

The life I was really living hit me when I woke up in a liquor store parking lot at nine in the morning, drinking out of an old beer can with a cigarette butt in it. Something was very wrong here. I was an alcoholic. I knew I needed to change my life.

But what was the first step?

Spiritual Sojourn

I thought of my time in heaven at Jesus's throne. With the angel, Mary, and all the witnesses, He had tried to get through to me, but it hadn't changed me. Yet He had planted a seed that I could nurture and grow—if I worked on my relationship with God, maybe I could feel connected to Him the way I did when I was a child. I decided I needed to spend time with myself—and God—at a spiritual retreat of sorts.

I went home and called my mom that hot August day.

"Please, you need to come get me," I said. While waiting for her to arrive, I packed a backpack. When Mom got there, I asked her to drive me to the desert and drop me off in a canyon. "Come back and pick me up in three days," I said. "If I'm not here to meet you, then assume I'm dead."

Of course Mom wasn't thrilled with the idea, but as I've explained, my parents lived under the philosophy of letting people fail with the hope that they would learn from the experience. They'd tell me not to do something, but after that, they'd step back. When I'd do the thing anyway and suffer the consequences, I'd sometimes ask them afterward, "Why didn't you stop me?" Their response was always, "Would you have listened?" And of course, the answer was always no.

The canyon I chose was a place I had played in as a kid. I left my food and supplies at the spot where my mom dropped me off and took only my tent to set up camp. My plan was to come back later for the rest of the supplies. It was so hot and humid, and I was so tired from the long walk and pitching the tent that I decided to go back for my food and supplies the next morning.

In the middle of the night, I heard loud music nearby. I worried that the people having the party would take my food, so I left my tent to get it. By the time I showed up, the partiers had driven away, but my food was still there.

On the way back to my tent, however, I got lost. As I wandered around, I ran right up on a rattlesnake. All I had with me was a little flashlight. I used the flashlight to find a rock to throw at the snake, and it slithered away.

Finally, I found my way back to my tent and zipped myself inside for the night. I wondered what to think of seeing a deadly snake on the first night of my spiritual journey into nature. I thought about how, during my near-death experience, God had shown me things in terms that I could comprehend, from a cartoonish devil to a silver angel. I wondered if now He was showing me the devil again in the form first presented to mankind in the Bible. I figured His showing me the snake was a sign that He wanted to talk, so that got the conversation rolling. In the tent that night, I made an agreement with God that I was going to change my life.

I could feel God's presence with me, assuring me of His love.

The whole reason I'd gone to the desert alone in the first place was because I knew I needed to get away from the bad influences in my life, to get completely away from alcohol and marijuana, which were so easy for me to get. I wasn't new to going cold turkey on either substance. My pattern had been to smoke and drink for a couple of weeks and then to take a week off. I didn't have withdrawal symptoms. This was not about drying out. This was about going out in nature to sit with God.

The next morning, I sat on a rock and started talking to God again, and I began to wonder if He was really there with me. Then, in the middle of this brown, dried desert, a vibrantly red bird landed right in front of me and sat there for a long time. I took that as a signal, as if God were telling me, "Yes, I'm here." I could feel His presence strongly and could feel Him speaking to me and reassuring me of His love.

As I spent time alone with God and my thoughts, I tried to remember everything I could about what had happened to me when I'd been taken to the hospital five years before. I wanted to try to make sure that I remembered it all.

By the time the three days were over, I'd lost a dramatic amount of weight from sweating so much. I'm five foot eight, and I went into the desert weighing about 125 pounds; I came out weighing only 110. But it wasn't just my body that was changed. I also felt like I'd signed a new contract. I decided to turn my life over to God. My end of the deal was that I wasn't going to let anything like that morning in the liquor store parking lot happen ever again.

Powerful Lessons

When I left the desert, I left my old life behind. I let my girlfriends have everything we owned and moved out of my house. I took my college entrance and civil service exams. I stayed in college only a year before I got a job as a roving security officer with a big company, and I got to work in lots of different environments, including hotels, apartment complexes, hospitals, and police stations.

I started thinking about where I was in my life and what I was doing with it. I decided it was no coincidence that, as a security officer, my job was to watch what was going on, essentially to be a paid witness. If I was a witness in my job, then I could also be a witness for God. I felt like He'd given me my marching orders and that it was time for me to do His will. *I am a Christian*, I decided. *There is no way I could not be.*

Over the next few years, as I spent more time pondering my near-death experience, I could see God working in my life. But it was hard to stay on the straight and narrow. In my thirties, I started working for a friend's rock and roll band as a technician. Given my struggle with alcoholism, it was not the best decision for me to get back into that sort of fast and free lifestyle.

Still, like most addicts, I thought I could handle the temptations of substances and women. I wanted to have both the wild lifestyle and the walk with God and tried to find a way to reconcile the two. Instead of running from the influences that tried to drive a wedge between God and me, I began praying for power—some type of power over my circumstances. I never specified what sort of power.

I was in my thirties by this point. Within a week of those prayers for power, I developed the same ability to feel other people's emotions the way I had when I saw things from the doctor's perspective in the hospital and the way I had felt others' emotions in heaven. That same extreme empathy. For about three weeks, I played around with this new "gift" before I realized it was too much for me. Here on earth, I could not handle such power. I was like a four-year-old child trying to drive a sports car.

Ideas would pop into my head that seemingly came out of nowhere. When I would mention them to people nearby, they'd wonder how I'd come up with an idea they'd just been thinking about. Soon, no one had to tell me which person the idea had come from—I just knew. I'd feel an emotion that someone else was feeling. I'd send a text or make a phone call, mentioning an event that popped into my head, and the person would respond, "How did you know I was just thinking about that?" This happened with not just one or two, but about fifty people. Or I'd go into a store and suddenly feel the emotions of everyone around me. It was so overwhelming that I couldn't even remember what I'd gone into the store for in the first place.

There were times during this period when I would sit alone and talk with God, asking Him any question I had, and He put the answers in my head immediately. I finally asked Him why He answered my questions so easily, and His response was, "Because you don't question Me." He answered me not in words but in thoughts that I recognized were not my own.

This sixth sense was like one of the other five senses in some ways. For example, if I tasted or smelled something, I would know where it came from. Similarly, when these thoughts and images and ideas would pop into my head, I could tell where they came from too.

I had to ask God to take this burden from me. I cried out to Him, "You're always there for me, and You're always helping me. You're always warning me about things. Why didn't You warn me about this?" I didn't really expect an

I finally understood that people have to fail on their own sometimes.

answer, but I got one. The Lord said, "Would you have listened?" It threw me into a flashback of times when my parents had said those same words to me in my youth.

I finally understood that people have to fail on their own sometimes. If you try to intervene, they'll either resent you for not letting them do what they wanted or blame you for their failure. Both God and my parents told me not to do things, but when I didn't listen, they were still there to help me pick up the pieces. When God took away the "power" I'd requested, it was a huge relief.

However, I wouldn't say that the absence of this empathy has made me just like everyone else. Sometimes things happen that I knew were coming. When Mary showed me the compressed vision of future events, I did not have context for them or know when they would happen, but there are times when they've come to pass. For instance, Mary had shown me a vision of myself lying in bed with a broken back, so I knew it was coming, but I had no idea how or when.

In 2012, I was by myself and was trying to move a stove up a flight of stairs. I lifted the stove up and took one step up when I felt searing pain. I fell on the ground in a squatting position and could not move. When I wound up lying in bed with a broken back, I realized I had seen this before: Mary had shown it to me.

A New Life

It is difficult for me to put into words the type of relationship I have with God today. At this point in my journey, I seek hands-on work from God and do as He asks. I consider this an assignment-based relationship. I am brought to people who are in situations that require things only I can provide as a conduit for God's work. I feel that it is not important where I am going as long as God is leading, so I just do as I am asked.

I feel that it is not important where I am going as long as God is leading.

I've learned from my near-death experience that knowledge can be a burden in addition to being a gift. God showed me a long time ago that my life of excess and extremes was not fulfilling, and now I live an entirely different lifestyle.

Mary had told me that my life would be over when I was forty-six—at least that's what I thought she meant when she said "forty-six." For years leading up to my turning forty-six, I expected that I would die at that age. That didn't happen, but I don't think Mary was wrong or told me something that wasn't true. In a sense, my life as I knew it did end when I was forty-six.

It was during that year that I left my position as a supervisor for the security company and moved to Mississippi to take care of my elderly mother, whose health had begun to deteriorate. When I left my job and moved (I have never married and have no children), I had no idea what I would do, but I found work installing alarms and electronic systems. I enjoyed it a great deal until I had to quit because Mom could not be left alone at all. I took over her housecleaning business since she could no longer manage it. My life now is a far cry from the wild and crazy times of my youth but comfortable nonetheless.

The way I see it, forty-six was not the end of my life but the beginning of taking care of my mom. I look at it as my chance to make my life right. In many ways, I feel like the mythological phoenix, rising from the ashes of my life into something new. I don't worry about the future; that's been one of the biggest gifts of my near-death experience. I know I can trust God to lead me, so I don't spend time worrying about the unknown.

I have faith in Jesus. To say that Jesus isn't the Son of God and my Savior would be like saying the sky is not above me. For me, it's undeniable. No matter what happens in my life, I never feel isolated or lonely because Jesus is my best friend. He is always with me. I let Him down earlier in my life, but I made a promise to Him that it won't happen again, and that's a promise I intend to keep.

My Life since My Near-Death Experience

Jeffrey Coggins

My NDE occurred in 1989 when I was nineteen years old. I'm in my fifties now, so it's been over thirty years since my experience. Almost none of it made sense right after it happened, but like a puzzle, it became clearer as I put together more pieces. My understanding of why I witnessed the things I did has also become clearer.

Q *What kind of reaction did you get when you shared your near-death experience?*

A I don't talk to many people about my NDE. The first time I actually shared my experience was when I posted it on a website about NDEs in 2012. I had been listening to a radio station late at night, and the guest was a guy who studies NDEs. He asked anyone who'd had such an experience to post their story to his website. I had already written down everything I could remember about my experience because I didn't want to forget any of it. So I pulled it out, edited it, and posted it. Since then, I've heard from others who have had an NDE, which has been a meaningful part of my life. I know that God has put these people in my path.

Sometimes I have mentioned parts of my story to specific people in reference to helping them deal with their problems, particularly if they are suicidal. But I've never really told the whole story because I don't like to talk about it. I'm afraid people will think I'm crazy once I tell my story. Talking about a near-death experience can be like talking about aliens or Bigfoot—people stereotype you.

Q What has been the biggest challenge in returning to an earthly life after your NDE?

A I think the biggest challenge was changing my lifestyle. I was "living the dream," as some people say. God didn't make me change my life or take anything away from me. I had to learn for myself that what I thought was good for me really was not.

Q Have the feelings and emotions you experienced during your NDE influenced your life? What feelings did you experience when you returned?

A I do have a greater sense of love and peace now. I felt a lot of love during the event itself, but I didn't accept it at the time. Afterward, I remembered the feeling but didn't want to accept it. I wanted to keep living a self-centered life. But after I went into the desert and spent time with God, I accepted the greater sense of love and peace as a gift. Now, all these years later, I still have those feelings, but they've been with me for so long that I worry that I take them for granted.

Q How does what you experienced during your NDE affect how you see your life and the world around you?

A Sometimes I feel like I've been handed an instruction manual for a machine, but the machine I'm supposed to operate is not the one described in the instructions. It's like I'm trying to apply heavenly principles to an earthly existence, which doesn't always work.

Particularly stressful situations, such as the COVID-19 pandemic and Hurricane Katrina, where the world seems to be falling apart, remind me of what I learned during my NDE—that everything will be okay. While everyone else is panicking, I'm not afraid. In troubling situations, I have a greater sense of reassurance because I have a greater connection to God.

Q *How did your NDE change your relationships with God and people around you?*

A I've never been able to deny that God has been part of my life, but after the NDE, I really had to acknowledge that He's always there. When I grew up, I had grandparents, but they lived far away, so while I technically knew them, I didn't really know them. I didn't have a close relationship with them. Before the NDE, it was like this with God and me—someone who is removed from your daily life versus someone who's actually with you all the time. God is no longer this remote being just in words or in writing; He's with me all the time, and if I make a mistake, I feel like I can see the disappointment on His face.

I have more compassion for people now and look for their soul, so that they are more than just a character to me. I don't make assumptions about people or stereotype them. I remember how brash and immature I was when I encountered the heavenly souls in my NDE, and I recall how patient and understanding they were with me because they realized I didn't have the experience and wisdom they did. I try to remember that people who frustrate me haven't had the same experiences I've had. Rather than give into frustration, I try to approach them with understanding and compassion, just like the heavenly souls did for me.

A Note from the Editors

We hope you enjoyed *Heavenly Encounters,* published by Guideposts. For over 75 years, Guideposts, a nonprofit organization, has been driven by a vision of a world filled with hope. We aspire to be the voice of a trusted friend, a friend who makes you feel more hopeful and connected.

By making a purchase from Guideposts, you join our community in touching millions of lives, inspiring them to believe that all things are possible through faith, hope, and prayer. Your continued support allows us to provide uplifting resources to those in need. Whether through our communities, websites, apps, or publications, we inspire our audiences, bring them together, and comfort, uplift, entertain, and guide them. Visit us at guideposts.org to learn more.

We would love to hear from you. Write us at Guideposts, P.O. Box 5815, Harlan, Iowa 51593 or call us at (800) 932-2145. Did you love *Heavenly Encounters?* Leave a review for this product on guideposts.org/shop. Your feedback helps others in our community find relevant products.

Find inspiration, find faith, find Guideposts.
Shop our best sellers and favorites at
guideposts.org/shop
Or scan the QR code to go directly to our Shop

Printed in Great Britain
by Amazon